Andrew Stanislav

In recognition of

Graduation with Distinction in
Urban & Regional Planning

Department of Geography

Miami University

2014

MIAMI UNIVERSITY: A PERSONAL HISTORY

Miami University: A Personal History

By Phillip R. Shriver

President Emeritus & Professor of History

Edited and with a Preface by
William Pratt, Professor of English

Miami University Press
Oxford, Ohio

Library of Congress Cataloging-in-Publication Data

Shriver, Phillip R. (Phillip Raymond), 1922 -
Miami University : a personal history / by Phillip R. Shriver : edited and with a preface by William Pratt.
p. cm.
Includes index.
ISBN 1-881163-28-8
1. Miami University (Oxford, Ohio) - - History. I. Pratt, William, 1927- . II. Title.
LD3241.M52S57 1998 98-6081
378.771'75- -dc21 CIP

The paper in this book meets the guidelines for permanence and durability of the Committee on Production Guidelines for Book Longevity of the Council on Library Resources.♾

Printed in the U.S.A.

9 8 7 6 5 4 3 2 1

Acknowledgment

This book was suggested by Dr. Anne Hopkins, Provost of Miami University, whose support has been essential to its completion.

Table of Contents

LIST OF ILLUSTRATIONS

Photographs courtesy of Miami University Archives (Bob Schmidt), Miami University Art Museum, and Miami University News Bureau.

Preface

by William Pratt

I first learned to love Miami history because of the late Walter Havighurst, honored colleague in the Department of English when I arrived on the Miami campus in 1957; I have come to love it even more because of Phillip Shriver, former President and later esteemed colleague in the Department of History, who has raised my appreciation of that history to a new level. I am grateful to them both, because if there is anything I treasure about Miami, it is its history. I started learning about it, as many others have, by reading various editions of *The Miami Years* by Walter Havighurst, and now—unlike many others who have been fortunate enough to take his course in Miami History—I have enriched my knowledge by reading transcripts of Phillip Shriver's lectures, which are here offered in the form of a book.

I freely admit that, thanks to what Walter Havighurst and Phillip Shriver have taught me about the institution where I have taught for forty years, I have come to love the Old Miami more than the New Miami—or perhaps I should say that it is the Old Miami *in* the New Miami I love, the small classical liberal arts college still making its presence felt in the midst of a large teeming modern multiversity. There is a difference between them, and the difference means that history matters here, more than it matters generally in this country. Americans have a national tendency to revere the future more than the past, with the result that, as Oscar Wilde once observed, "The youth of America is its oldest tradition. It has been going on now for three hundred years."[1] We are always making ourselves over, it seems, and we tend to regard the new as necessarily better than the old. Socially and politically, perhaps,

[1] Oscar Wilde, *A Woman of No Importance* (1892)

the case can be made for American progress, but educationally the past matters more than the future. Education gathers and transmits the wisdom of the past in order to generate wisdom in the present, because there is no other way for wisdom to grow, and by that simple measure the Old Miami is still an essential part of the New Miami. If you read this overview of nearly two centuries of educational metamorphosis, by a professional historian who served 16 years as president of Miami University, I think you will understand why.

Not that Phil Shriver is backward-looking or reactionary, I hasten to say, because he is thoroughly optimistic and progressive in his outlook, and his infectious enthusiasm for Miami as an institution, past, present, and future, is evident on every page of this history. But higher education—not only at Miami but at every university—was higher when it offered the rigorous, if limited, Classical Humanities curriculum of Greek, Latin, and Mathematics, than it has been since. The main difference between the Old and New Miamis, or pre-Civil War and post-Civil War Miami, can be summed up in the contrast between the Classical Humanities and the present Miami Catalogue. Notice I said higher; I did not say broader. In terms of breadth, and the range of practical skills it offers, certainly the New Miami is far superior to the Old Miami. And the newer education serves many more students, since the Classical Humanities curriculum was too demanding to be mastered by more than a small minority—imagine learning enough Greek and Latin to read Homer and Virgil while learning enough calculus to master Newtonian Physics! No wonder there were at most 250 students on campus before the Civil War, because they all had to "major" in the Classical Humanities; today, there are over 16,000 students on the Oxford campus alone, and no two of them have to take the same curriculum; they enroll instead in hundreds of courses fulfilling dozens of majors.

There is another major difference between the Old Miami and the New Miami which Phil Shriver clearly shows: the Old Miami was dominated by Protestant Christianity led by Classical Humanists, while the New Miami has become a mainly secular and scientific institution. A succession of ordained Presbyterian ministers were presidents of the Old Miami, while the presidents of the New Miami—including Phil Shriver himself—have come from a variety of academic fields, English Literature and Chemistry and History and Political Science and Zoology and Botany and Physics. William Holmes McGuffey, the most famous member of the Old Miami faculty, besides serving as Professor of Classics and writing the McGuffey Readers which educated generations of Americans, preached regularly in Presbyterian churches in and around Oxford. Professors at the New Miami have been business and educational and political consultants, and have written books on a huge diversity of subjects, but few of them have preached in local churches, or would be respected by other faculty members or students if they did.

In view of such vast differences, both academic and religious, it is simply not conceivable that the Old Miami could become the New Miami, yet this history tells us it did, for Miami as an institution of higher education has changed drastically in the course of two centuries, but it has remained Miami University in more than name. The fascination Phil Shriver shows for Miami history enables him to describe the institution in all its multiple personalities without losing sight of the continuity that makes it so venerable, a true Alma Mater in the original, formative sense of a "Spiritual Mother," as well as in the later, more congenial sense of a "Mother of Fraternities" and the even later, more pejorative sense of a "Mother Miami." Miami is both the venerable old and the controversial new, and its history is ongoing; what is most important is that it *has* a history, therefore a reputation and a character as a *uni-*

versity, that is to say, a unity amidst all the complexity.

This book is about what makes a university possible in the first place and what keeps it going despite all the radical changes in its makeup. Only a historian of Phil Shriver's experience could see the continuity while recording in lively and often humorous detail the changes that have taken place since 1809, when the charter for "The Miami University" was issued by the State of Ohio. That original document stated that a "good education" should promote "virtue, religion, and morality." Who in today's university would list even one of those goals as central to the institution? We read instead in the current catalogue that the Mission of Miami University is chiefly "to individualize the educational experience" of its students, by offering them a variety of courses to choose from; in other words, despite the mention of "values" as an important part of the Miami mission today, the means of education have largely become the ends. Phil Shriver is not blind to the gradual subordination of ends to means in the two centuries of higher education here recorded, but he takes the generous view that what is vital about a Miami education survives, and that students are being as well equipped now to manage computers and take leading positions in the American corporate technocracy as they were a century ago to enter the professions and take leading positions in the earlier American political republic. One student of Classical Humanities at the Old Miami, Benjamin Harrison, became President of the United States; his equivalent in the New Miami would no doubt be a Business major who becomes the CEO of Procter & Gamble and then of General Motors, in other words, John Smale.

Continuity amid change is one of Dr. Shriver's themes in his history of Miami University, and another is creating and maintaining a healthy learning environment. The Miami campus is one of the glories of American higher education, an ever-expanding array of mainly red brick buildings in the Colonial or Neo-Georgian architectural style, surrounded by well-kept lawns and shaded by huge trees, and from the time when it was three buildings in the woods Miami has kept its serene and peaceful prospect for generations of faculty and students to enjoy as their field of contemplation. What takes place inside the buildings is a reflection of what exists outside; nature and man are potentially in harmony. That William Holmes McGuffey could become "Schoolmaster to the Nation," while he was a Classics Professor seated at his octagonal desk in a study overlooking the center of the Miami campus, provides early proof that the environment for learning works. Later proof could be cited in the many volumes of regional history, including one of the best university histories, *The Miami Years,* produced by English Professor Walter Havighurst from his study looking into the woods of Shadowy Hills on the north side of the Miami campus. But the loyalty of thousands of Miami students past and present to their campus scene is the best proof that the environment is right for learning whatever one sets out to learn.

I call this book "A Personal History" because it comes from the lectures presented by President Emeritus and Professor Phillip R. Shriver for many years at the university, and the stamp of his personality is on every page of it. All I have tried to do in editing these lectures on Miami history is to condense them, by reducing (but not eliminating) the digressions and repetitions normal in oral presentation, to make a continuous narrative, without losing the flavor of Phil Shriver's unique individual voice. It is his book, not mine, as I probably needn't say, since the reader is bound to hear him speaking throughout. Those acquainted with *The Miami Years* may be surprised at how little overlapping there is between the two accounts of Miami history, but Phil Shriver gives Walter Havighurst credit for making the main distinction about Miami history: there was an Old Miami which ended after the Civil War, and a New Miami which began late in the nineteenth century and continues to thrive late in the twentieth century. In its first phase, the Old Miami was a classical liberal arts college on the frontier, and in its second phase, the New Miami has become a "Public Ivy," a premiere national university in a country where the university is a shrine of American democracy, international in its influence—we even have a European Center in Luxembourg—and universally admired for its atmosphere of serious learning. The history of Miami University is finally a great American success story, and Phil Shriver as both President Emeritus and Professor of History is the right one to tell it in his inimitable way. From here on, this book is all his.

CHAPTER I.

THE HERITAGE OF OLD AND NEW ENGLAND

In my view, Walter Havighurst's *The Miami Years*[2] is one of the finest college histories that has ever been written. The author taught in the Department of English on this campus from the late 1920s until 1969, a period of some 40 years, and in the course of it he wrote 36 volumes on a host of subjects, most dealing with regional history. When Walter Havighurst looked at the history of Miami University, he quickly saw that it was divided into two main parts: Old Miami and New Miami.

Old Miami extends from 1809, when the university was first chartered, through 1873, following the Civil War, when the University was forced to close its doors. It had quite simply become bankrupt, because it had an all-male student body, and since most of the students fought in the war, on both the Union and the Confederate sides, and the war lasted from 1861 to 1865, there were four years with few students to provide the fees. It is a striking fact that when the Civil War began, there were 512 American colleges, but soon after the Civil War was over, only 104 were left. Over 400 colleges closed their doors during or immediately after the war, and Miami was one of them. It took us 12 years to pay off the bills; when we reopened our doors in 1885, the period we call "New Miami" began and it has continued ever since.

Fortunately, it was in this period that women were admitted, and we became co-educational. We had opened our doors for the first time early in the century, when there was not a college in the world admitting women. Like all colleges of that period, Miami was a school for men only. But soon after the war, we became co-educa-

[2] First written and published in 1959, Miami's Sesquicentennial Year, by G.P. Putnam & Sons of New York, with a second revised edition in 1969, and a third updated edition in 1984.

tional at "New Miami," and we have been co-educational from then on.

So the history of Miami University divides neatly into two parts, the Old Miami and the New Miami, just as noted by Walter Havighurst in *The Miami Years.* But there is much more to the story than a simple chronological division, for Walter Havighurst did not begin his history of Miami with the year of our charter, 1809, but with the 14th day of February 1811, when there arrived in the national capital of Washington, D. C., the strange figure of a solitary man on horseback, dubbed by Professor Havighurst, "the beggar on horseback." He was a Methodist minister, the Rev. John W. Browne, who was the first employee of Miami University, and who went off on a mission of fund-raising, soliciting money needed to start a new school in the beech woods of southwestern Ohio. The Rev. Browne believed in starting at the top, and so he made his way to the White House, where he interviewed the President of the United States, James Madison. He also interviewed the Vice President, a man with the prophetic political name of Clinton. President Madison and Vice President Clinton were contacted by Rev. Browne on his initial visit to the national capital, and though they did not offer him support, he was not discouraged, but went on raising funds to start a university on the Western frontier.

An earlier historian of the university, Alfred H. Upham, also a Professor of English, was commissioned in 1909 by the Board of Trustees to write the first book-length history of Miami University, which he called *Old Miami: The Yale of the Early West.* Alfred Upham, later to become the President of Miami, began his history on the first day of November 1824, with the meeting of the original faculty of three men including the President, Robert H. Bishop, as they were preparing to begin classes for an initial student body totaling 20.

And so the years 1811 and 1824 have been selected by

earlier historians of Miami as the true beginning years, but legally the university began with the passage of an Act of Charter by the General Assembly of the State of Ohio on February 17, 1809—the very week when Abraham Lincoln was born in Kentucky. It was this legislative act which created *The* Miami University (we soon dropped the article *The* from our name), designating it to be located in the area of the Miami River valleys in southwestern Ohio.

But there was an even earlier point of origin, for on the 5th day of May in 1792, George Washington, the Father of His Country and first President of the United States, signed into law, during his first term in office, a measure setting aside a college township of land in the area called the Symmes Purchase of the Miami Valleys. This township was to be set aside for the support of an academy or other institution of higher learning, and it is in the college township that Miami University exists today.

Thus there are at least four different years that can be claimed historically for the beginning of Miami University: 1792, 1809, 1811, or 1824. But I prefer not to choose any of them. Instead, I propose to go centuries back, indeed a whole millennium, to the ninth century A.D., in order to affirm that Miami University was not created in a vacuum. Miami University was created following centuries of experience in higher learning, first in Europe, then in other continents around the globe, and it was out of this long tradition of higher education that our university would emerge in 1809 by legislative charter, and then in 1824 by opening its doors and offering its first classes.

We know that the word "university" comes from the Latin word *universitas,* meaning "a community, a corporate body." We also know that some time late in the ninth century (late in 800 A.D., though we don't have a specific date for it), a group of young men who wished to become physicians employed a seasoned veteran to pass onto them his accumulated wisdom, garnered through decades of practice, so that they would not have to repeat his mistakes at the expense of their patients. The medieval university traces its origins to a medical school, and I think we can all understand the reasons why. You could find out through trial and error what worked and what didn't for the patients who suffered because of your lack of wisdom—untold agony perhaps, and even, at worst, burial. These aspiring young doctors agreed that it made sense to learn from the experience of others, so that they would not have to repeat earlier painful mistakes.

When you think about the origin of the university, you realize that we are the only species of life born into a state of history: we are able to learn from those who have preceded us and to benefit from the experience of our forebears. The university is a transmitter of knowledge from an older generation to a younger generation, each new generation passing on what it has learned from the experience and wisdom of the past generation. Virtually every class on a university campus is a history lesson, whether the subject is called chemistry or physics or English Literature. Through various subjects, knowledge from the past is transmitted to the present for the benefit of the future. No human being has to start by learning how to take two stones and make a spark to start a fire; instead, the human being born today starts with the computer, and if my grandchildren are any example, they'll start very quickly with their computer games and take it from there. So, back in the ninth century A.D., a group of young men who wanted to become physicians said, "Let's bring an experienced practitioner into our midst. Let's learn from him what we can for the benefit of our patients." And from that simple desire to learn from past experience came the university as we know it.

It was Salerno, on the southern coast of Italy, later the site of a World War II beach-head, that housed the first recorded *universitas:* a single room, a handful of students, a single teacher, no library, no laboratory—the first college classroom. The concept of *universitas* remained Italian, and the next university—some say it was really the first—was established in Bologna in northern Italy. This venerable university started as a school of law in the first years of the twelfth century. Then the university idea moved north and west into France where, in 1150, a group of French students hired their own instructors in the city of Paris, to found what was later called the University of Paris. By the year 1208, statutes were issued using that name, but in practice, the University of Paris had been underway since 1150.

Then seventeen years later, in 1167, a group of English students studying in Paris wondered, "Why shouldn't we have our own university in England? Why should we have to cross the Channel and come all this distance to learn in a foreign country?" At a place on the Cherwell River where, at one time, oxen had forded the river, English students in 1167 established the first English university at Oxenford, or Oxford as it would soon be called. The Romans, who had conquered Britain long years before, had called the place Oxonia, and so the students and faculty of Oxford University like to call themselves Oxonians. You sometimes hear that name used for the residents of Oxford, Ohio, who are "Oxonians," too, by virtue of the old Latin word used by the Romans.

Thus, the first English university was established at Oxford in 1167; soon there would be a second university at a place where the bridge crossed the River Cam, or Cambridge. It was established in 1209 at the very place where the Romans had earlier built a fort they called "Cantabrigia," and so the students of Cambridge University are called Cantabrigians. I have a colleague in the History Department at Miami who is a Cantabrigian, a graduate of the University of Cambridge, and who teaches in two universities: at Miami in the fall, at Cambridge in the spring. Cambridge was to become the second great English university. Both Oxford and Cambridge developed the college system, with halls of residence emerging as colleges that had their own separate facilities. University College was founded at Oxford as early as 1249, followed in 1263 by Balliol College, then in 1264 by Merton College, and today there are thirty-five colleges and five halls comprising Oxford University.

The colleges occupied opposite sides of the main thoroughfare in Oxford, England, which was named "High Street." When my wife and I visited Oxford several years ago, we crossed High Street as we visited the various colleges and picked up a little colored brochure in which we read this paragraph:

> Nowhere is the magnificence of Oxford better exemplified than in High Street, the thoroughfare which runs east and west from Magdalen Bridge to the city centre at Carfax. Described by Carl Philipp Moritz, who visited Oxford in the year 1782, as "the longest, finest, most beautiful street in all of Europe," it is certainly the most famous and most admired High Street in all of England.

Oxford, England, has its High Street. And Oxford, Ohio, has its High Street. The principal east-west thoroughfare in the two academic towns bears an identical name, not by accident.

As Oxford University emerged as a cluster of colleges and halls on opposite sides of High Street, so Cambridge followed, with Peterhouse College in 1284, Michaelhouse in 1323, King's Hall in 1326, Pembroke in 1347, Corpus Christi in 1352, and Emmanuel College in 1584 (I will say more about this college later). The English university was a collection of colleges, a pattern which would eventually influence the American university.

In time, a number of other universities emerged across Europe. Following Salerno and Bologna in Italy, Paris in France, Oxford and Cambridge in England, the University of Valladolid was established in Spain in 1346, the University of Florence in Italy in 1349, the University of Vienna in the Austrian Empire in 1364, Heidelberg University in Germany in 1385, St. Andrews University in Scotland in 1411, Glasgow in 1452, and Edinburgh in 1582. Our first Miami President, Robert Hamilton Bishop, was educated at the University of Edinburgh, and we have faculty on campus at present who are graduates of the University of Edinburgh.

However, because our heritage in the United States is essentially English (that is, in culture, customs, law, language, and government), we derive most of our influence from the English universities of Oxford and Cambridge. The English heritage of higher learning was transmitted to the North American colonies in the seventeeth and eighteenth centuries, with nine New England universities bearing the stamp of Oxford and Cambridge. Miami University has an inheritance that begins in the Old World and was transmitted to the New World through colleges established in the thirteen original colonies. These colonies became the United States at the close of the colonial period, following separation from England in the American Revolution. For 176 years we had been part of the British Empire, from Jamestown in 1607 to the Treaty of Paris in 1783, which recognized our independence from Great Britain. Miami was one of the very first universities to come out of our newly won independence in the early republic of the United States of America.

The English inheritance had a number of features, the first and most evident of which was the predominance of religion. The old universities came into being primarily to educate a learned clergy. The clergy were expected to be the teachers in each community and the transmitters of culture, and they had to be learned, even if no one else was. It is significant that of our nine colonial American colleges, eight were church-related. Only one was not connected with a church, and that was the Philadelphia Academy, as it was called in the late 1740s; today, it is known as the University of Pennsylvania. The other eight were all church schools, and their primary function was the preparation of a learned clergy to play leading roles in the newly established colonies of Great Britain.

Another inheritance which passed from the old English universities to the new English universities in America was residentiality. Students were expected to spend all their time studying, and so they were obliged to leave their homes and take up residence in the university, making a full-time commitment to the mastery of subjects in which they were instructed. So like the old universities in England, the nine colonial colleges and the first of the new colleges in the early republic, including Miami University, were set up to be residential universities.

Another heritage was transmitted from the old university to the new: red brick architecture. We call it "Georgian," an expression which, when I was growing up, I thought of as geographic, referring to a big plantation house where they served mint juleps on the veranda in late afternoon. But I found out that Georgian referred to a period of time when a line of Kings named George ruled over England—George I, George II, George III, and George IV. George III was the most notorious of them, because he was the poor fellow against whom we rebelled in 1775, and against whom Jefferson directed his Declaration of Independence on the Fourth of July in 1776. What I learned was that the predominant style of architecture in England in the period of the Georges, or the Hanoverian Kings of England, was the red brick style. Look out of any window on the Miami campus and you will see the Georgian style of architecture, millions of red bricks out there. We have some buildings that contain as many as eight million red bricks, quite a bundle.

There is another inheritance from the old England of the Georgian period to the new England of the Puritan period which has been passed on to this university, and that is the concept of a four-year undergraduate educational experience. The years all had familiar names: freshman, sophomore, junior, senior. Alas, in recent years, the word "freshman" has fallen out of favor. We now speak rather clumsily of "first-years." When all the students were males, there was no problem with freshman; it was simply a word. I don't want to seem old-fashioned, but I still have no problem with "freshman." And I do treasure "alma mater," which is a feminine term, implying the all-embracing, loving university as a family of students, which leads us to speak of "Mother Miami." I hope we don't become so carried away with political correctness that we remove all terms such as "freshman" that carry any gender connotation.

So a four-year undergraduate curriculum was transmitted from the old England to the new and then to succeeding colleges and universities. Then there was the curriculum itself. The Classical Humanities curriculum was in vogue in the English universities and in most of the other European universities as well. The foundation of the classical curriculum was Latin, the language of scholarship. It was a unifying force: you could be in different countries, but every educated person would speak the same language, Latin. You could have a variety of publications in a host of vernacular languages, but the language of scholarship was Latin: all the texts were written in Latin, the basic supplementary works were in Latin, and the mode of instruction in the classroom was Latin.

Until the middle of the twentieth century, the prime requisite for admission to college was a firm grounding in Latin, both written and spoken. I know whereof I speak, because I am somewhat older than the students I teach. When I went to Yale in 1940, I had to have three years of Latin on my record, and I had to take the college boards in Latin. When I got to Yale, I had to pass a course called "Classical Civilization," the history of Greece and Rome. One of the welcoming addresses was given to us in Latin, and at commencement time, the principal oration was in Latin. When I got my diploma from Yale—which, incidentally, was printed on the skin of a sheep, who had given his all so that I could have a diploma of sheepskin—every word was in Latin, even my own name in Latin. I remember that when I came to Oxford, Ohio, as late as 1965, the Roman Catholic church of St. Mary's, one of the principal churches in town, still said the Mass in Latin, and biology courses continue to use Latin names for plants and animals.

Latin was the main foundation of the classical curriculum, but there were other courses, for instance Greek and Hebrew—not modern Greek, ancient Greek, and not modern Hebrew, ancient Hebrew. In your freshman year, you had these three ancient languages, Greek, Latin, Hebrew. You also had logic, which today is part of what we call philosophy. You also had rhetoric, which is part of what today we call Freshman English and Speech or Communication. Not quite all has disappeared of the classical curriculum, though most of it has.

If you survived to the sophomore year in the classical curriculum, you continued Greek, Hebrew, and logic, and you were introduced to what was called natural philosophy. Today it would bear closest resemblance to physics. By your junior year, you would be introduced to metaphysics. Metaphysics could be likened to speculative philosophy, seeking to explain the nature of being and the nature of the universe by trying to answer such questions as "Why are we here on earth?" and "What purpose is there behind it all?" and "Is there any meaning to life other than simply existence?" Metaphysics sought to answer those most basic questions. Then there was moral philosophy, a grab bag of what today we would call the humanities and the social sciences, embracing history, ethics, political science, economics, and sociology. Such was the four-year undergraduate curriculum we inherited from Old England: the three years I have enumerated, plus the fourth, the senior year, in which you had primarily Latin and review. Before you could go out into the cold cruel world you had to have one final update in Latin, plus more Greek, more logic, more natural philosophy or physics, and higher mathematics. These were the components of the classical curriculum.

The classical curriculum was taught at Emmanuel College, part of the English Cambridge. Emmanuel was established in 1584, and is a major bridge from the old England to the new. It was founded in the late sixteenth century, following the English Reformation, which was begun under King Henry VIII and continued under his daughter and successor, Queen Elizabeth I. (The present Queen Elizabeth is Elizabeth II). The first Elizabeth was on the throne in the late sixteenth century and ruled with an iron hand. Like her father and predecessor, Henry VIII, she affirmed that she was the head of the English church after the break with Rome. The English church was still quite Roman in many ways, but in one major respect it was Protestant rather than Catholic: the monarchs in England declared they were the head of the church, not the pope in Rome.

It was out of this ferment in England caused by the Reformation that a movement called Puritanism emerged, a movement within the Church of England that sought to purify it of remaining Roman Catholic doctrine, dogmas, and traits. On the Cambridge campus, Puritans in particular challenged the wearing of academic regalia, the mortar board, the robe, the hood, because they maintained it was too similar to the garb of the priests. Of all the colleges at Cambridge, Emmanuel was the most puritanical, and there were even some Puritans who held that there was no way to purify the church from within. They called themselves Separatists, and they argued for a complete break from the Anglican as well as the Catholic church. They were a minority group of Puritans, a more radical fringe element, but it was a group of Separatists who boarded the ship, *Mayflower,* in Holland, and crossed the Atlantic to land at Plymouth in present-day Massachusetts in 1620. We commemorate their landing every year when we celebrate Thanksgiving.

This small group of Separatists soon were followed by a much larger wave of Puritans who came to settle the whole of the Massachusetts Bay colony, including Boston and its suburbs. By the early 1630s, there were 10,000 Puritan colonists. They determined that they, too, had a need for a church-related college to prepare a learned clergy for the colony of Massachusetts. Among the 10,000 people in the Massachusetts Bay area, there were ninety college graduates. Seventy of the ninety came from Cambridge University, only twenty from Oxford. And of the seventy college graduates from Cambridge, thirty-four came from Emmanuel College—almost half. Hence, their concept of what the church college should be like in Massachusetts was Emmanuel College at Cambridge University. One of the Emmanuel graduates was a young clergyman named John Harvard.

When my wife and I were in England a few years ago, we stopped at Stratford-on-Avon because of our interest in William Shakespeare. But as we were passing down the main street of Stratford, I looked up and saw a plaque on the second floor of a house marking the birthplace of John Harvard, a young Puritan clergyman and a graduate of Emmanuel College, Cambridge. When John Harvard died, still in his early 30s, in 1637, he bequeathed his entire library of about two hundred books along with half his worldly possessions to the newly founded college, and in gratitude to him the trustees voted to name it Harvard University. Two years later, they voted to change the name of the community in which it was located from Newtown to Cambridge, Massachusetts. So Emmanuel College exerted a primary influence in educating the leaders of the Massachusetts Bay colony.

Thus, very early in American history, the name of one of the two principal English universities was pre-empted by a school called Harvard and a town called Cambridge. But the name of the other was still available, and when in 1809 a new school bearing the name of an Indian tribe was chartered for the beech woods of southwestern Ohio, the town where it was located was named Oxford. In 1810, the decision was confirmed by the General Assembly in the State of Ohio, when it decreed that the school to be called The Miami University should be located in a town called Oxford. This would be the first Oxford in North America. Today, there are eighteen Oxfords in Canada and the United States, but we're the oldest. Oxford, Ohio, was the first American college town to honor the English university town and so we can claim priority in the use of the name. Old England became New England, and old Oxford became new Oxford; thus was the medieval European university heritage transmitted from the Old World to the New.

Chapter II

A TRIBE NAMED MIAMI, A TOWN NAMED OXFORD

No, Miami University did not begin in a vacuum, but as part of a continuum. Centuries of experience led to the formation in medieval Europe of an institution called *universitas,* a community of scholars, that is, of teachers and learners, through whom one generation could transmit to a new generation the accumulated wisdom of the past.

The university as an institution was born in the ninth century on the southern coast of Italy; later in the Middle Ages, it moved to northern Italy, thence to France and across the English Channel. American higher education was transmitted directly from England to New England, during the 176 years when we were part of the British Empire. Colleges were established in the thirteen British colonies on the eastern seaboard, beginning in 1636 with the one called Harvard, founded by graduates of Cambridge, especially of Emmanuel College, a college singularly favorable to Puritans, the group that sought to purify the English Church of its remaining Catholic doctrines and dogmas.

When these Puritans came to the New World, they saw the need for a church school to prepare a learned clergy, since in their view society looked to the clergy for leadership. If the clergy were learned, it was believed they would transmit their learning to the faithful of their congregations in their ministries. So it was no accident that of our nine colonial colleges, eight were church-related. Harvard was most closely related to the Puritans, who in the course of the seventeenth and eighteenth centuries would evolve into the sect called the Congregationalists.

Today, in the late twentieth century, the successor church to the Congregationalists calls itself the United Church of Christ. Harvard was located initially in a suburb of Boston called Newtown, but the name was changed to Cambridge in 1638, two years after Harvard was founded, in recognition of the fact that most of the Harvard heritage, including the faculty and the curriculum, came out of Cambridge University in the mother country. The name Harvard was bestowed upon the school in 1639, when a thirty-one-year old Puritan clergyman, John Harvard, died and left half of his estate of 800 English pounds currency and his entire library of 260 volumes to the new school. It was in gratitude for the generous will of John Harvard that the trustees voted to name their school Harvard University, giving the oldest American university the name of Harvard in the town of Cambridge, Massachusetts.

Thus, the first American college was Puritan; the second was Anglican. Today, the successor to the Anglican Church, or Church of England, is called the Episcopal Church, and the college it founded in 1693 is still called William and Mary. The Virginia colony was older than the Massachusetts Bay colony, since Jamestown had been settled in 1607, while Plymouth was not settled until 1620. In the Virginia colony, an early effort had been made to establish a church school, and in fact as early as 1619, a subscription was launched, contributions were received and funds were assured, to get a new school underway. Unfortunately, an Indian attack on the Jamestown colony wiped out the principal prospective contributors. As a consequence, the donations were never received and a church school in Virginia was postponed from decade to decade until, finally, in 1693, a college was established. It would be named William and Mary in honor of the then-reigning English monarchs, King William and Queen Mary of the House of Orange, who occupied the throne of England. Earlier in the seventeenth century, there had been a revo-

1. Seal of Miami University, designed in 1826 by the first President, Robert Hamilton Bishop, and Professors John Annan and William Holmes McGuffey

2. Robert Hamilton Bishop, first President of Miami University, 1824-40, graduate of the University of Edinburgh and ordained Presbyterian minister (Oil Portrait on Canvas, 1829-30, painted by Horace Harding, commissioned by the Miami Union Literary Society, courtesy of the Miami University Art Museum)

3. George Junkin, second President of Miami, 1841-44, later President of Washington College in Virginia and father-in-law of General Stonewall Jackson

4. Tombstone of George Junkin in Stonewall Jackson Cemetery, Lexington, Virginia, naming him (incorrectly) as the Founder of Miami University

5. William Holmes McGuffey, Professor of Classics and Editor of the McGuffey Eclectic Readers, which made him famous as Schoolmaster to the Nation in the nineteenth century

6. William C. Anderson, Fourth President of Miami, 1849-54, who restored good feeling to Miami after the Snowball Rebellion of 1848 and reinstituted college fraternities on campus (Oil Portrait by unknown American artist, c. 1850, courtesy of the Miami University Art Museum)

7. Charles Elliott, Professor of Classics, resident advisor in the original North Dormitory later named Elliott Hall

8. Orange Nash Stoddard, Professor of Science, resident advisor in the original South Dormitory later named Stoddard Hall (Oil Portrait on Canvas, 1883, by Michael Strieby Nachtrieb, courtesy of the Miami University Art Museum)

9. Old Main, later named Harrison Hall, principal academic building on the Old Miami campus; begun in 1816, it survived until 1958, when it was replaced by a new Harrison Hall

10. Chapel in Old Main, where compulsory daily prayers were held for students and faculty at Old Miami, resumed for a time at New Miami (Postcard by Frank Snyder)

11. Andrew Dousa Hepburn, first Professor of English and last President of Old Miami, 1871-73, sworn foe of co-education, reappointed at New Miami as first Dean of Liberal Arts (Photograph by Frank Snyder)

12. Robert White McFarland, Professor of Mathematics at Old Miami, rehired as first President of New Miami, 1885-88, then fired by the Trustees because of his long-standing feud with Professor Hepburn

13. Banner in 1892 announcing candidacy of Benjamin Harrison for President and Whitelaw Reid for Vice President: the only time a national party's candidates for U.S. President and Vice President were graduates of the same university

14. Slant Walk, leading from town to campus, preserved as an open space by successive Boards of Trustees

15. President Ethelbert Dudley Warfield, (second from left in front row) 1888-91, and his "Dude Faculty" from Eastern universities; hired when only 27, he introduced the sport of football to Miami,

16. Miami Football in 1895, a new game brought from Princeton by President Warfield, who in 1888 refereed the first Ohio football game, Miami vs. Cincinnati (Photograph by Frank Snyder)

lution in England of Puritans led by Oliver Cromwell, which brought the monarchy to an end with the beheading of King Charles I. But there was a Restoration of the monarchy under Charles II and the House of Orange succeeded the House of Stuart. William and Mary, the new monarchs, would be honored not only with the name of the second American college, but with the name of what would become the capital of the Virginia colony, Williamsburg.

If you have visited what is today called Colonial Williamsburg, you have seen the College of William and Mary at the far end of the Duke of Gloucester Street, and you have gazed at its principal building, which is called the Sir Christopher Wren Building. It was named for the most celebrated of the British architects of the seventeenth and early eighteenth centuries, who received a commission in London to draw the plans for a new college building in Williamsburg. That building, erected in 1695, is today the oldest academic building in America. But you don't have to visit colonial Williamsburg and walk the mile-long Duke of Gloucester Street to see what the Wren Building looks like. You have only to cross the Miami campus to the northeastern corner and see the Marcum Conference Center, which is a handsome replica of the Wren Building, erected in 1980.

The College of William and Mary was named for the English sovereigns and sponsored by the Church of England. Though its original building was three times consumed by fire and three times rebuilt, there are still some of the original bricks in the Wren Building. It was at the College of William and Mary that the first American law school was established, and some of its outstanding graduates in the pre-Revolutionary era were Thomas Jefferson, James Monroe, and John Marshall, whom we honor among the founding fathers of this country.

The Greek letter societies that we call fraternities and sororities were also initiated at the College of William and

Mary, with the chartering in December, 1776, of Phi Beta Kappa, the first Greek letter fraternity on an American campus. Phi Beta Kappa began as both a social fraternity and an academic honorary, and for its first twenty-five years, it combined the two, but then it dropped the social function, and since the early nineteenth century it has been exclusively an academic honor society. In the academic world, Phi Beta Kappa has been synonymous ever since with high academic achievement, while other Greek letter societies have flourished on American campuses as primarily social institutions.

The College of William and Mary, chartered in 1693, became the second oldest American college, followed in 1701 by the third oldest, Yale, located in New Haven, Connecticut. Interestingly, Yale was founded to counter the influence of Harvard, since many Puritans in Connecticut were alarmed that Harvard was drifting too far to the left and they felt it was too liberal. To provide a balance, the Conservative Puritan, now Congregational, clergymen got together in 1701 and started a new school in Connecticut. To this day, many think Yale has tended always to be a bit to the right of Harvard, and Harvard, conversely, a bit to the left of Yale. Yale's first campus was in Killingsworth, Connecticut; then after half a dozen years it was moved to Saybrook, also in Connecticut, and thence in 1717 to New Haven, where it has stayed. The name of Yale was given to the school by its board as a consequence of another benefactor, Elihu Yale, a merchant and political leader. Elihu Yale had made a small fortune in Boston, received a commission to serve as Governor of Madras in India, made a further fortune in Madras, then went to London and added to his fortune. In 1718, Elihu Yale gave the princely sum of 582 pounds, English currency, to the new school in Connecticut, in gratitude for which the trustees named it Yale University. Its students have ever since liked to refer to themselves as the sons (and, since 1969, daughters as well) of old Eli, that is, the descendants of Elihu Yale. What is more important is that Yale began as a conservative Puritan or Congregational institution, one of the many church-related colleges in the American colonies.

The fourth university to be established in the colonies was the only one that was non-church related. We know it today as the University of Pennsylvania, but it began in 1740 as a charity school for indigent youth, publicly supported by the city of Philadelphia. On its board of trustees was the most eminent American intellectual of the eighteenth century, Benjamin Franklin. Franklin was responsible for raising this school from its rather lowly beginnings as a charity school for indigent youth into a public academy with high academic standards, which it became in 1749. Six years later, in 1755, and again with Franklin's urging, college courses were introduced. The public academy of Philadelphia changed its name in 1791 because the overwhelming number of its students were already collegiate, not just preparing for college, and so it is known now as the University of Pennsylvania. But it remained the only one of the first nine American colleges which was secular and not religious in origin.

After the University of Pennsylvania came Princeton University in 1746, started in Elizabethtown, New Jersey, with the backing of the Presbyterian Church. The two largest Christian denominations in the colonies were Congregational and Presbyterian, followed by the Church of England, the Anglican or Episcopal Church. The dominance of Presbyterians reflected the large numbers of Scottish and Scotch Irish emigrants to America. They established a college in the New Jersey colony with the specific purpose of educating ministers in the Presbyterian or Calvinist faith. Princeton's original name was the College of New Jersey, but after half a dozen years in Elizabethtown, the college moved to Princeton, New

Jersey, still with the name of the College of New Jersey, and so in 1896, the trustees finally acknowledged its common name and officially named it what it has been ever since, Princeton University.

The Presbyterians of Princeton in New Jersey were followed by the Anglicans of Columbia in New York City, who in 1754 founded the fifth American college in our largest metropolis. Leadership and initial support for Columbia came from the Church of England; however, its charter specifically provided that adherents to four other denominations could also serve on its board of trustees. So, though it was Anglican primarily, it was also interdenominational. It became known as Columbia University, though its official name at the outset was Kings College. Its seal bears the crown of a king to this day. But when, in the 1770s, the American Revolution broke out against the tyranny of King George III—at least that was what the revolutionary leaders claimed—King's College was understandably closed and did not reopen until after the revolution, when it was given the new name of Columbia University. Its name derived from Christopher Columbus, the Genovese captain who discovered the New World, whose reputation at that time was generally associated with liberty and freedom, as in the popular anthem, "Columbia, the Gem of the Ocean." Kings College dropped any suggestion of the monarchy by adopting the new name of Columbia, which suggested freedom, democracy, and a new nation.

A decade after the founding of Columbia, the first college in Rhode Island was established, the one we know today as Brown University. It began its existence as the Rhode Island College in Warren, Rhode Island, founded by Baptists but opening its doors to all students. It had Baptist Church support, but would nonetheless be interdenominational—some might say even nondenominational, but still it was a Christian college. It moved early from Warren to the largest city in Rhode Island, Providence. In 1804, it took a new name, Brown, to recognize its benefactor, a Revolutionary War veteran and graduate by the name of Nicholas Brown, and Brown University it has been ever since.

Brown, chartered in 1764, was followed two years later by a Dutch Reformed Church school that today we know as Rutgers. It was founded in New Brunswick, New Jersey, to provide a church-supported school for the preparation of ministers of the Dutch Reformed faith. We forget sometimes how extensive was Dutch influence throughout the colonial period. But remember that New York began as a Dutch colony called New Netherlands and its principal city was called New Amsterdam. The Dutch settled on both sides of the Hudson River in New York and New Jersey, giving rise to such odd names as Weehawken and Hoboken, and claiming at least three American presidents for the Dutch: Martin Van Buren, Theodore Roosevelt, and Franklin Delano Roosevelt—all were of Dutch ancestry.

Closer to home, a Dutch immigrant named Zachariah DeWitt came out of Hudson Valley Dutch stock on the New Jersey side to build the first home in the Talawanda Valley in 1804. The DeWitt log cabin still stands, and it is now the oldest building on the Miami campus; in fact, Zachariah DeWitt helped to determine the exact location of Miami University, as we shall see.

Rutgers was called Queens College when it was founded in New Brunswick in 1766, but years later, in 1825, in recognition of the generosity of a Dutch Reformed descendant of the Revolutionary War veteran and philanthropist, Henry Rutgers, the school changed its name from Queens College to Rutgers University. Much later, in the 1950s, the State of New Jersey began appropriating public funds for its support, converting it from a private, independent university to a public, state-supported institution. Today, its name is officially Rutgers, The State University of New Jersey. We owe one of our recent presidents to Rutgers, since Dr. Paul G. Pearson came to Miami in 1981 after serving as the Executive Vice President and Acting President of Rutgers.

The ninth and last of the colonial American colleges we know today as Dartmouth in Hanover, New Hampshire. However, as we have seen with many of our colleges, Dartmouth didn't begin with the name Dartmouth and it didn't begin in Hanover. It started as an Indian school in Lebanon, Connecticut, chartered with the support of the Congregational Church, in other words out of Puritan ancestry. It was the creation of Eleazar Wheelock, who sought to establish a school in New England primarily for the education of Indian youth. This was not the first time such an effort had been made. Harvard, as early as 1654, had established an Indian College in Cambridge, Massachusetts, as part of Harvard University. Though a number of Indians did matriculate at Harvard, only one graduated, and Harvard came to the conclusion that an Indian college was not really feasible. The Indian college established by Eleazar Wheelock in Lebanon, Connecticut, also suffered from lack of students, and so in 1769, the trustees determined to move it out of Connecticut into New Hampshire and open its doors to all students. With the move came a new name, Dartmouth College, recognizing the particular leadership and philanthropy of the Earl of Dartmouth, who was then serving as Chairman of the Board of Trustees.

So, of the nine colonial colleges, three came from Puritan—that is, Congregational, Calvinist, latterday United Church of Christ background—Harvard, Yale, and Dartmouth; two were of Anglican background—William and Mary and Columbia; one was of Presbyterian background—Princeton; one was Baptist—Brown; and one was Dutch Reformed—Rutgers. Only one of the nine was non-sectarian, fully public, with no church relationship or affiliation of any kind—the University of Pennsylvania. All nine were well established by the eve of the American Revolution, but at that time, interestingly enough, in a total population of more than three million inhabitants of the thirteen colonies, there were just under three thousand college graduates, fewer than the number who presently graduate in one year from Miami University. The nine colonial colleges did not turn out mass numbers of graduates. Their enrollments were small, but their influence carried far beyond their numbers, because the graduates included many of those who were our Founding Fathers—just think of Jefferson, Monroe, and Marshall, all of whom graduated from the Law School of the College of William and Mary.

When the Revolution began in 1775, the college graduates of America were at the forefront of the military, political, and religious leadership in the nation. It wasn't expected in 1775 that there would be a new nation, but after the 4th of July 1776, and the Declaration of Independence, nationhood became the main objective. The American Revolution began in 1775 as a protest against British imperialism, against the subordinate role played by the thirteen colonies in the British Empire. But in fact a new nation had already emerged. In the 176 years of colonialism, there had been not only English but Irish, Scotch, Scotch-Irish, German, Finnish, Swedish, French, Spanish, and Dutch immigrants, all beginning to fuse into a new breed called American. They spoke English, but there was a pronounced difference in the way they spoke it and the way the English spoke it. Local pride resented the continued English reluctance to give full rights of citizenship, including the right to vote, to British subjects on this side of the ocean.

For eight years, the American Revolution was fought against British dominance, and then, in September 1783, a treaty was drawn up in Paris to bring it to a close. Great Britain finally had to acknowledge that the thirteen former colonies were now the United States of America. They also acknowledged that the western boundary of the United States of America was to be the Mississippi River, meaning that the new nation of thirteen United States would begin life with colonies of its own. The thirteen colonies were all on the Atlantic seaboard, but now they had an empire that went westward from the Appalachian mountains to the Mississippi River, a larger expanse of land than had been colonized so far. Immediately, the new nation had thrust on it in the wake of independence the need for a colonial policy.

To the two great documents of freedom which emerged in the Revolutionary period and immediately thereafter, the Declaration of Independence and the Constitution, a third great document should be added, the Northwest Ordinance of 1787, which established the most liberal colonial policy the world had ever seen. This Northwest Ordinance said that the territory north and west of the Ohio River was not to remain subordinate for long. From it would come three to five states; not less than three, not more than five. These states would come into the Union on the basis of equality with those already in the Union. The specific words in the Northwest Ordinance were that they would be equal in every respect to the thirteen already in the Union. Here was a mother country stating at the outset that it wouldn't even use the word "colony"; it would use the word "territory." It wouldn't use the word "colonist"; it would use the word "settler" and make that synonymous with "citizen." Here was a new mother country saying that the colonies, which were her territories, would be extensions of the mother country. Here was a plan by which the mother country could grow from thirteen to twenty to thirty to forty to fifty states, and amazingly, the plan is still in place. It's been followed all the way, not only through the Northwest Territory to the Mississippi River; it has been followed all the way to the Pacific Ocean and outward across the ocean to Hawaii and Alaska. When my grandfather graduated from high school, there were thirty-five states in the Union. When my dad graduated, there were forty-five. When I graduated, there were forty-eight. When my son graduated, there were fifty. Am I going to tell you that when my grandson graduates there will be more than fifty states? I don't know. But there could easily be fifty-one or fifty-two, if we added the District of Columbia and Puerto Rico. So the plan is still in place. If you want to see what the Northwest Ordinance symbolized in terms of its importance, look at the American flag: fifty stars, each the same size. Not thirteen big ones (the mother country) and a lot of little tiny ones (the colonies), but fifty equal stars. That was the significance of the Northwest Ordinance. And what did it signify for Miami University?

Look at Article III of the six Articles which make up the Northwest Ordinance, which could be called a Bill of Rights for those who had crossed the mountains and the river to come into this land, rights such as freedom of speech, of the press, and of assembly. Before there was ever any Bill of Rights for the American Constitution, there was a Bill of Rights for the people who would live in the new territories it governed. One of the Rights was to live in freedom. Article VI declared the first prohibition against slavery in the new nation, thus making part of the country free when the rest was not, long before the Civil War. The Northwest Ordinance stipulated that north and west of the River Ohio, no one was to live in bondage to anyone else. Then there was Article III, the famed education provision: "Religion, morality, and knowledge being necessary to good government and the happiness of mankind, schools and the means of education shall forever be encouraged."

Yes, education was encouraged by the Northwest Ordinance, and so was freedom of worship—not freedom *from* religion, but freedom *of* religion. Morality was held to be as important as learning for human happiness. Freedom, our Founding Fathers said, would hinge on religion, morality, and knowledge, together the bulwarks of education. They realized that if they could get anyone to cross the mountains and the river to come out here to this wild country and settle down, there had to be some assurance that their children would not suffer and that educational opportunities would be such as they were used to on the East Coast. It would be a powerful inducement to settle here if children had the same opportunity for education they had in the original colonies, now the United States of America.

Those who wrote the three founding documents of the country, the Declaration of Independence, the Constitution, and the Northwest Ordinance, were educated men. Though there were fewer than 3,000 college graduates out of more than 3 million living in the colonies, those 3,000 represented the leadership. Of the fifty-five men who traveled to Philadelphia to devise the Constitution under which we are still living, thirty-four were college graduates. In other words, more than half the delegates to the Constitutional Convention were college graduates, even though college graduates represented less than one-tenth of one percent of the whole population. A similar majority of college graduates prevailed among those who had written the Northwest Ordinance in the Congress in New York a few weeks earlier. Of the thirty-four graduates in Philadelphia, ten were graduates of Princeton, five were graduates of William and Mary, four were graduates of Yale, three were graduates of Harvard, two were graduates of Columbia, two were graduates of Pennsylvania, and eight others were graduates of such older universities as Oxford and Glasgow in Europe. So twenty-six of the framers of the U.S. Constitution were graduates of the colonial colleges, and eight were graduates of the colleges of the Old World. Certainly these thirty-four knew the importance of education, and they knew that if this new democracy was going to work, if this new territory was going to emerge as new states, there had to be enlightened leadership. So they wrote that "schools and the means of education shall forever be encouraged," and clearly they meant it.

The Northwest Ordinance was written in 1787, the very year when a group in Massachusetts organized itself into a land company to settle the area around the Muskingum River. Headed by Rufus Putnam, it would be called the Ohio Land Company. The name Putnam is still potent, because the Lieutenant Governor of the State of Ohio in 1998 is Nancy Putnam Hollister, a direct descendant of Rufus Putnam, and she still calls Marietta home. The Ohio Land Company was awarded a contract for a million and a half acres in southeastern Ohio with the provision that two townships would be set aside for the support of an academy or other institution of higher learning. The university that owes its origin to this provision is called Ohio University at Athens, located in the heart of the Ohio Company lands.

Just a year later, in 1788, a New Jersey group headed by a former Congressman and Judge, John Cleves Symmes, was given a patent from Congress for the settlement of a million acres in southwestern Ohio, between the two rivers named for the Miami Indian tribe, the Great Miami and the Little Miami. This patent would be called the Symmes Purchase or the Miami Purchase, and it too stipulated that a township would be set aside for the support of an academy or other institution of higher learning. Today on the campus of Miami University, which was the beneficiary of this provision, there is a residence hall in the East Quad named for Symmes. If anyone could be called the symbolic Father of Miami, it would be Judge Symmes. He was the actual father-in-law of William Henry Harrison, one of the Presidents of the United States, and his great-great-grandson was Benjamin Harrison, another U.S. President. To honor the Harrison connection, we have Harrison Hall in the middle of the campus, and we also have the Anna Symmes Harrison Room in the Shriver Center. Through the Symmes Purchase of 1788 the new nation was assured that there would be an academy or university in this section of the new state of Ohio.

As the Ohio Company would establish Marietta as its first permanent settlement, the Symmes group would establish Cincinnati in 1788. They would also establish Columbia (where Lunken Airport is today) and North Bend (where the Great Miami River enters the Ohio). As you may know, Cincinnati was not initially called Cincinnati. It was called Losantiville, which lingers today in a golf course by that name, but Losantiville was an artificial creation. There was a Latin scholar by the name of Filson among the original settlers, and he said, "If we need a name, let's turn to Latin and call the place L for the Licking River, os for the river mouth, anti for in front of, and ville for village." The Licking River flows northward through Kentucky, right through present-day Covington and Newport, and enters the Ohio across from what is today downtown Cincinnati. So, Cincinnati was to be the ville anti os (the mouth of the ell, the Licking River). The first Governor, Arthur St. Clair, arriving in Losantiville in 1791, said, "This is a horrible name. There is no magic about it. There is no ring about it. It grates against the ears." He was a member of the respected Revolutionary War Association of Officers called the Society of Cincinnati, named for the old Roman patriot, Cincinnatus, who had dropped the plow and taken up arms in defense of Rome. Arthur St. Clair declared, let this place be called Cincinnati, and that is the name that stuck. Thus Marietta, Cincinnati, Columbia, North Bend, and other towns came to be established along the Ohio River, as the settlers purchased land from the Ohio Land Company and the Symmes Purchase.

There were, however, earlier settlers, native American tribes who had called this area home for generations, who objected strongly to the invasion of their territory by new inhabitants. Among the tribes taking their stand against the white settlers was the Tribe Miami. Principal among the leaders taking this stand was one called Mishikinakwa, the Little Turtle of the Miami people. Mishikinakwa was born at Blue Lake in northeastern Indiana, not far from the largest Miami town, Pickawillany, near what is now Piqua in what is still called Miami County, Ohio. Growing up, he was known as the son of Ashikinakwa, the Turtle. The women of the village thought he was the spittin' image of his dad, and so they called him Mishikinakwa, the Little Turtle. He was Little Turtle all his life, even to the ripe old age of eighty.

Little Turtle complained that the Indians did not have any representation in New York or Philadelphia when the white men made their decision to settle in the new territories. He said the land was parceled out from one group of Europeans to another or to their descendants on this side of the ocean. The Americans saw the Indians as allies of their enemies, the British, in the American Revolution. And, indeed, most of the Indians who fought in the war fought on the side of the British. To the Americans, the Indians had lost because the British had lost. But in the second sentence of Article III in the Northwest Ordinance there was a statement that the land which belonged to the Indians was not to be taken from them, except by "just and lawful wars" declared by Congress.

Well, it didn't take long for a "just and lawful war" to be declared by Congress in 1790. It was President Washington's Indian War, prompted by the actions of the

Indians, under Little Turtle, who began to conduct raids on the new settlements in the Ohio Valley, forcing George Washington to call out the troops. In opposition to the armies of the new United States, Mishikinakwa established what came to be known as the Miami Confederacy, made up not only of the Miamis (which included six subgroups bearing such names as the Weas, the Piankashaws, the Kilatikas, the Mengakonkias, the Pepikokias, and the Atchatchakangouans) but those called the People of the South Wind, literally, the "Southerners," the people called Chaouanons (Shawnees). There were the People of Fire, the Potawatomis. There were the fur traders of the North, the Ottawas. There were the Kickapoos, the Wyandots, the ones called Hurons by the French because they wore their hair high in the middle, roach-like, shaved on the side. When the French saw these folk they called them "hures," meaning "bristle heads" because of their war-locks. The English called them Wyandots, the French called them Hurons, but they were the same tribe. The Delawares (or Lenapes) joined the Confederacy, and together they fought twice under Mishikinakwa. They defeated the armies of the United States for the first time at Kekionga, where the headwaters of the Maumee are to be found today in northeastern Indiana, the site of present-day Fort Wayne. Three rivers were once called Miami: the Miami of the Lake, the Little Miami, and the Great Miami of the Ohio. To reduce the confusion, the name Miami of the Lake was changed to Maumee, as it is today. On the banks of the Wabash, which rises in Ohio, at the site of present-day Fort Recovery, a second defeat, the worst ever inflicted on an American army by a force of Indians, was inflicted by Little Turtle, leading the Miami Nation and the Miami Confederacy, on the army of Governor Arthur St. Clair. It was worse even than the defeat by Indians of the forces of British General Braddock in the French and Indian War.

Finally, at the place called Fallen Timbers, in the valley of the Maumee, near present-day Perrysburg, a crushing defeat was administered by Anthony Wayne to the army of the Indians then led by the Shawnee Blue Jacket. Out of this defeat at Fallen Timbers in August 1794, came the Treaty of Greenville in 1795, by which the Indians surrendered title to two-thirds of the present State of Ohio, including the grounds of Miami University. Everything east of the Cuyahoga River, the Portage Path, and the Tuscarawas River to Fort Laurens, (the only Revolutionary War fort on Ohio soil); south of a line connecting Fort Laurens to Fort Loramie and Fort Recovery; and east of a line running sharply southward from Fort Recovery to the mouth of the Kentucky River where it empties into the Ohio was voided of Indian title and opened for settlement. Within eight years, there was such a rush of settlers that Ohio would come into the Union as the first State carved from the Northwest Territory under the principles of the Northwest Ordinance of 1787. In 1996, places as far apart as Cleveland, Dayton, and Chillicothe celebrated bicentennials that began with the Treaty of Greenville. The end of the Indian war had opened up the land for permanent settlement.

As for the Miamis, they did not call themselves by that name. They called themselves Tawee, meaning the cry of the crane. Miami tradition has it that in the dim, dark past, the Miamis were at one time attacked by Cherokees from the south and a Miami village was about to be destroyed as Cherokee warriors slipped up for the attack in pre-dawn darkness. The village was located adjacent to a large marsh of shallow water. As the Cherokees approached, they startled a large group of sandhill cranes. These large birds, four and a half feet high, rose from the water calling tawee, tawee, tawee—their alarm cry when frightened. Their cry awoke the Miamis inside the village who took their bows and arrows and at once defended themselves against the attacking Cherokees. And, according to Cherokee tradition, the Miamis wiped out all but one Cherokee, who limped back to his village one hundred or more miles away, and who reported that as the Cherokees were about to attack, the Miamis were transformed into great water birds who rose from the water and fell upon them, destroying all but one. But, according to Miami tradition, it was the alarm cry of the sandhill crane that had saved them. Thus "Tawee," the cry of the crane, became the name of the people.

How, then, did they come to be called the Miamis? Well, up in east central Wisconsin, as we know from the first historical records about the various tribes, French Jesuit missionaries contacted the Chippewas, known as the Ojibways in Canada. Chippewas, living to the west of the Door Peninsula, surrounded by the waters of the Green Bay, called the people living out on the Peninsula the Oumamik. Later, French reports back to Montreal convoluted the word Oumamik to Oumami and then to Oumiami, and finally to Miami. It was Father Jacques Marquette, the great explorer, who in the year 1673 was the first to spell the word "Miami." He was the one who selected two Miami warriors to be his guides on his epoch-making trip from Green Bay to the Fox River to the headwaters of the Mississippi and down the Mississippi, claiming the whole valley for France. Father Marquette said he selected Miamis as his guides because they were the bravest and the smartest, the ones who never came back from an expedition without success, the handsomest of all the Indians he had encountered. The description is a compliment to those who call themselves Miamis, even to this day. Because he called them "Miamis" when he selected them to be his guides, they have been the Miami Indians ever since.

The history of Miami University as an Indian tribal name thus starts at Green Bay on Lake Michigan, and moves down the shoreline to the southern extremity, where in 1690 Chikagoua was established as a Miami village. Today we know it as Chicago, Illinois, the third largest city in the USA. The Miamis named it Skunktown in their language, not because of the striped polecat with the strong odor, but because of the plant, the skunk cabbage, the odor of which permeated the place. The Miamis moved from northern Illinois to Indiana, from Indiana to southwestern Ohio, and that was where they were when the Northwest Ordinance of 1787 opened up the new territory. They took the lead in resisting white settlement of their lands, and their resistance ultimately determined that a university in Oxford, Ohio, would bear their name, as a mark of admiration for the people who had called this home, who loved it as those of us who live here today love it, still bearing the name Miami.

CHAPTER III

MIAMI OF OHIO, FLORIDA, OR OKLAHOMA?

It was in the middle 1930s that the President of Miami University, Dr. Alfred H. Upham, received a letter of inquiry. He was in what was then the Administration Building, which we now call Hall Auditorium, and the letter was from the President of the University of Miami in Coral Gables, Florida, asking him to consider a change of name. The President of the University of Miami in Florida suggested that because his university was in a much larger metropolitan area and was destined to grow rapidly, as it had been doing for a number of years since it was chartered in 1925, confusion about the names could be avoided if Miami University in Oxford, Ohio, would simply change its name. I don't have before me a copy of Dr. Upham's response. Suffice it to say, he did not take kindly to the suggestion that a university chartered in 1809 should change its name in favor of a university chartered in 1925. He probably pointed out that in 1809, Florida was still part of the Spanish Empire and was not even part of the United States. There was no Miami at all in Florida in 1809, nor would there be until 1896.

So there are still two universities called Miami: the one we know best is in Oxford, Ohio, not in Miami, Florida. Of the two Miami Universities, one was chartered as The Miami University, the other as the University of Miami. For four decades, we called our athletic teams the Redskins, while the other Miami calls its teams the Hurricanes. Our nickname at least indicated that the name Miami comes from an Indian tribe, a tribe that still exists.

The Hurricanes are perhaps a somewhat less troublesome nickname than the Redskins, even though I understand a few years ago someone seriously objected to calling the other Miami teams the Hurricanes, arguing that there should also be "Himicanes" to make up for the unintentional sexism. Anyway, a hurricane is a storm, not a tribe, and hurricanes may be called by either male or female names: one of the more destructive recent hurricanes was called Fran, but to make up for it, an even more destructive one was called Hugo. Thus, those who care about gender equity should at least be satisfied in the case of hurricanes.

The Miami University that is located in Oxford, Ohio, has an enrollment of just over 16,000 students, with 5,000 more at the Middletown and Hamilton campuses and the campus in Luxembourg, for a grand total of over 20,000 students. The University of Miami down in Coral Gables, Florida, had at last count a little more than 13,000 students, making it somewhat smaller than the Miami in Oxford, Ohio, but the other Miami has achieved a certain national prominence because of the prowess of its athletic teams, particularly in the sport of football.

There is no doubt however that in the origin of the name, Miami, we have priority over Florida. I find in a book entitled *College Names, Their Origins and Significance,* by Albert Keiser, a derivation of the word Miami from a Chippewa term meaning the people who live on the peninsula, a clear reference to what we have already spoken about, the Indian tribe that came from Wisconsin to Indiana and Ohio, where they gave their name to three rivers. The Miami of the Lake, as it once was called, is today the Maumee River, while the Miamis that empty into the Ohio River are still the Little Miami and the Great Miami. It was simple proximity that gave Miami University in Ohio its name.

But what about that other Miami? How did it get its name? People from Florida ask, in all innocence, "How did you ever get our name way up there in Ohio?" It doesn't seem to matter when we say, "No, it's the other way around," because they just laugh and say, "Well, everybody knows Miami is a Florida name." Some even say "It's a Seminole word meaning sweet water." I looked up the Seminole word, and found it had one M in it, the fourth letter of the word, but otherwise there was nothing in the word to suggest that it was in any way related to Miami. I have even heard a less likely story of the origin of Miami as a name in Florida. There is supposed to be a legend about an Indian Chief who admired a beautiful maiden, and said "How beautiful you are." You'll laugh at her supposed reply, "My, am I?" But rather than strain credulity that far, let's turn to a book entitled *Florida Place Names*, by Allen Morris, printed by the University of Miami Press in Coral Gables, Florida. Such a book should certainly be trusted to give an authoritative account of the origin of Miami as a name.

Under Miami, Dade County, we read that the true derivation of the name Miami in Florida is a mystery. *Florida Place Names*, published by the other University of Miami, says that Miami is not a Seminole word, since no words have been found in the Seminole language that mean "sweet water" and sound like "Miami." The book goes on to say that the word Miami comes from the Chippewas, a group of northern Algonquin Indians, who use it as a name for the people who live out on the point, meaning the peninsula, and it is the Chippewa word that accounts for the name of Miami University in Ohio. A writer for *The Miami Herald,* John Pennekamp, says his research indicates that Indian trade routes might have brought the Chippewa word into Florida, but he goes on to say that "Today's Miami [Florida] was chartered in 1896 with the coming of the Florida East Coast Railway." That railway was not constructed by Chippewas; it was built by Ohioans. Ohio real estate investors came out of Dayton and Hamilton, out of Montgomery and Butler counties, and built the Florida East Coast line, connecting one city, Daytona, with the city to the south of it, Miami. Dayton, Ohio, is located in the Miami valley, and there should be no doubt where the names Daytona and Miami came from. The developers of the railroad connected the two towns: so much for the name Miami in Florida.

The word Miami is thus not a mystery after all. It is a Chippewa word meaning people of the point or people of the peninsula. In the Chippewa tongue the word was Oumamik for those who lived on the Door Peninsula surrounded by the waters of Green Bay in Lake Michigan. When the first Jesuit missionary, Father Gabriel Dreuillettes, came to the Green Bay area to establish a mission in 1658, he learned for the first time of the Oumamik. He spelled it Oumamik in his report to his superior in Montreal in the St. Lawrence Valley. A decade later, another Jesuit missionary, Father Claude Allouez, in his report on a mission established at what is now Green Bay, referred to the People living out on the Door Peninsula as the Oumiami.

The first to use the name of Miami as we know it today was Father Jacques Marquette, the renowned French explorer who made a canoe trip in 1673 from the Green Bay on the Fox River to the headwaters of the Mississippi, then traveled down the Mississippi hoping to reach the mouth of that great river and claim the whole valley for France. He took as his guides two Miami warriors, and in his journal, he spelled their name Miami. In French, he might have spoken of his friends as "mes amis," but that's not the way he spelled it. He used the Chippewa word, converting it from Oumamik to Miami, thus completing its transformation into the familiar name we use for Miami University. He admired the courage and comeliness of the Miamis, and so he selected two of them to be his guides. His word Miami was not theirs, but it remains the name of the Indian tribe that never called themselves the Miamis.

Instead, they called themselves the Tawee, meaning the cry of the crane. They were comparing themselves to the great water bird which we call the sandhill crane, an impressive creature that stands some four and a half feet tall and has a wingspread of about the same dimension. It is a large and handsome bird, once found in abundance in the marshlands of the upper lakes. To the Miamis, their totem was the crane, the water bird that had saved them, and so they took as their name Tawee, the cry of the crane.

The Chippewas and the French called them Miamis. But the English tried in the eighteenth century to spell the name as they heard it from the tribe, and they came up with "Twightwee." As we know from American history, at the close of the French and Indian War in 1763, the French were driven out of North America. French-Canadians would remain, but New France was at an end. England would take over Canada and the French holdings in the Mississippi Valley. Though the English triumphed, the French place names remained and so, too, the names given by the French to the Indians, including the Miami. I think we can be glad the French names prevailed, for can you imagine being students or faculty at a university called Twightwee? Or can you imagine telling your friends, when they ask where you are going over the Christmas break, "Twightwee Beach down in Florida"? Or would you want to sing that beautiful ballad "Moon Over Twightwee"? No. Miami has a certain alliterative charm lacking in Twightwee. And it has spread across the land, not only in Florida and Ohio but in scores of places in Indiana, Wisconsin, Michigan, and Illinois, as well. Ohio is brimming with Miamis. There are three rivers called Miami or Maumee, a Miami derivative, a county called Miami, towns called Miamiville, New Miami, Old Miami, Miamisburg, Miamitown, and a university called Miami. The name Twightwee has all but disappeared from the map. For a time we had a Twightwee Lodge here in

Oxford, part of the Arrowhead Lodges off Chestnut Street. And there is still an unincorporated village of Twightwee in northeastern Hamilton County, in the Loveland area, where a Totes plant is located today.

The Totes Company as you know makes rain gear—pop-up umbrellas, galoshes, overshoes, and raincoats. I stopped one day at the Totes store in Twightwee and asked the clerk, as I bought a pop-up umbrella, if she could tell me something about Twightwee, the little town in which she lived. She shook her head and said, no, she had always wondered about that name, here on the banks of the Little Miami River. I had to explain to this citizen of Twightwee what the name signified, that Twightwee was in fact the English name for the same people the French called Miamis. Twightwee has virtually disappeared, and I think all of us can be glad that Miami remains.

The Miamis who moved into western Ohio in the mid-eighteenth century left their footprints across the land. They were the warrior tribe who took the lead in resisting European-American settlement in the Ohio Valley after the Revolution. Under their leader, Mishikinakwa, the Little Turtle, the Miamis put together the Miami Confederacy to keep the land forever Indian. Twice under Little Turtle, they won significant victories over American armies, first in the battle of Kekionga, or Fort Wayne, and second, in the Battle of the Wabash, where Fort Recovery is to be found today. The latter battle on November 4, 1791, resulted in the worst loss ever sustained by an American army against American Indians. Not even Custer's Last Stand at the Little Big Horn suffered the number of casualties sustained by the army under General St. Clair at the hands of Little Turtle and the Miami Confederacy.

A third army was sent against them by President George Washington, under the command of General Anthony Wayne, and this time, in the Battle of Fallen

Timbers in August 1794, the Miami Confederacy was at last defeated. It should be pointed out that before the battle, Little Turtle counseled peace, urging his fellow Indian chiefs to accept the terms offered by General Wayne and avoid what he fully believed would be a disastrous defeat. He was right. He counseled peace, but the others shook their heads and refused to follow him. The Shawnee leader, Blue Jacket, succeeded Little Turtle in the position of leadership and it was Blue Jacket who led the Indian forces to disaster at Fallen Timbers.

In the peace treaty which followed, the Treaty of Greenville in August of 1795, it was stipulated that two-thirds of what we call Ohio today would be voided of Indian title. All of this area of southern, eastern, and western Ohio was stripped of any further Indian claim. Eventually, with the Treaty of Fort Industry (where Toledo is today) signed on the 4th of July, 1805, the Indians ceded to the United States the rest of the Western Reserve. Then, in successive treaties at St. Marys, Brownstown, Michigan, and the Maumee Rapids, what remained of the Ohio country was removed from Indian title. The Treaty of Greenville had said that the land west of the Cuyahoga would remain Indian forever, but forever lasted only ten years. It was not the happiest chapter in our history, for it led to the decision of President Andrew Jackson to remove the Indians altogether from eastern states. The Federal Indian Removal Act of 1830 called for the removal of the tribes east of the Mississippi to new lands west of that river. What followed was known as the Cherokee Trail of Tears, but the Miamis also experienced a trail of tears, since they were one of the last Indian tribes to leave the East.

In the Miami Removal of 1846, the trail of tears went by canal boat. Canal boats assembled at Peru, Indiana, in what is still Miami County, Indiana, and loaded the last of the Miami tribe aboard, then moved by the Wabash Canal to the Miami and Erie Canal from Defiance southward, and proceeded on five canal boats, passing along the way what had been the largest of the Miami towns, Pickawillany, near present-day Piqua in Miami County, Ohio. The Miami Trail of Tears continued via canal boat to Dayton, Middletown, Hamilton, and on to Cincinnati.

In Hamilton, Ohio, on October 12, 1846, a young lad nine years old stood on the canal banks and watched the procession of canal boats going by, each laden with Miami Indians. Many were in blankets, feathers, and fur robes, with bows and arrows at their sides. Years later, grown to manhood and recognized as America's foremost man of letters, William Dean Howells would write a book he called *Stories of Ohio,* recounting his memory of the exodus of the Miami Nation in 1846. He recalled thinking as they passed that they were leaving the land forever. But events proved him wrong, for we have a larger Miami Indian presence today on the Miami campus and in many places in Ohio and Indiana than we had in 1846, 150 years ago. The Miami footprints are still seen across the land.

When the Miamis were removed from their native lands, they were sent to Kansas. Canal boats took them to steamships on the Ohio where they were shipped to St. Louis. On the Mississippi at St. Louis, another steamship would take them north to the Missouri River, then west on the Missouri River to the Kansas Territory where a reservation of half a million acres awaited them. The Miami Nation would be in Kansas only seventeen years when they were moved again. The Territory of Kansas was to become the State of Kansas, and the tribe was moved out of Kansas to what was called the Indian Territory. We know it today by the name of Oklahoma. Interestingly, Oklahoma means "Red People" or "Redskins," but it is an Indian name and so it is not controversial. In Oklahoma the Miamis were put into the northeastern corner of Indian territory where soon a settlement emerged called Miami. It is now a town which is the gateway to the Indian country of Oklahoma. And it is where the Tribe Miami maintains its headquarters today. The Tribe Miami, located in Miami, Oklahoma, is made up of the descendants of those who were forced out of their Indiana and Ohio homes in 1846.

There is also a second group of Miami people, the Miami Nation of Indians of Indiana, with headquarters in Peru, Indiana. Miami removal commenced there in the fall of 1846, but the Miami Nation of Indians of Indiana is not federally recognized, and has not been for 100 years. They lost recognition in 1896. Not all the Miamis were moved out of Indiana and Ohio. This group in Indiana today represents those that were permitted to stay behind, many because they were principal land owners, others because they were acculturated, already living in effect the Euramerican way of life. Many had intermarried with other races, primarily white, and they were permitted to stay behind. They would ultimately be rejoined by some who left Kansas and Oklahoma to come back to their ancestral homes. They lost federal recognition in 1896 in large measure because the federal government believed they had resisted moving; they hadn't been forced to move, and so had not truly suffered as those who had been compelled to move had suffered relocation in Kansas and then Oklahoma. The Miami Nation of Indians of Indiana continues to press for federal recognition, and my own hope is that they'll get it eventually, though the outcome remains in doubt.

At Miami University today, we have representatives from both groups of Miami Indians, the Oklahoma group and the Indiana group. The university's formal relationship has been with the Miami Tribe of Oklahoma, the one which is federally recognized. It's a relationship that goes back several decades and was centered originally on an agreement about the use of the word Redskin. We had worked out agreements in 1972, 1988, and 1991, but in the summer of 1996, the Miami Tribe of Oklahoma requested that we drop the Redskin nickname. I myself have championed the use of Redskin for our athletic teams, but I have also said for years that the day the Miami Tribe asked the University to change the name Redskin, I'd be the first to make the motion. I truly believe the University should not continue to use it if the Miami Tribe does not endorse it. We have had very strong, very cordial relationships with the Tribe and its Chief Floyd Leonard. The Chief's son is a member of our faculty; the Chief's grandson is a member of our student body. We're proud of the fact that we have a number of Miami Indians with us today.

The Miamis and the other tribes defeated at Fallen Timbers in 1794 agreed in the Treaty of Greenville to cede two-thirds of Ohio, and in succeeding treaties they lost the remaining northwestern third of the state. After the Treaty of Greenville, with the Indian wars at an end, there came a flood of migration into Ohio. Recently, bicentennials have been held to celebrate in communities all over Ohio the opening of the land after the Treaty of Greenville. In Cleveland and Dayton, Chillicothe and Youngstown and Zanesville, one after another, bicentennials have been held and will continue to be held for the next several years. The rush of migration to fill up the void created by the ceding of Indian lands was so great that by 1803, Ohio had entered the Union as a state. It was the first to be carved out of the old Northwest Territory. Ohio had achieved the minimal population requisite for statehood, which was the size of the smallest state in the Union. After statehood was granted to Ohio in 1803, Article III of the Northwest Ordinance came into force, stating that "religion, morality, and knowledge being necessary to good government and the happiness of mankind, schools and the means of education shall forever be encouraged."

Right away, an effort was made to start a university in southeastern Ohio. It was chartered as the American Western University in 1803, but the charter was rescinded in 1804 and was replaced by a new one on February 1804, which chartered The Ohio University, using the name of the new state. Then, on February 17, 1809, a second university was established in the new State of Ohio, carrying out the mandate of Article III of the Northwest Ordinance, and this university was named The Miami University. The article *The* is in our name, as it was in the name of The Ohio University, but neither school has chosen to use it. Some universities do use the article *The* in front of their name, but we haven't used it, probably because we feel we are old enough not to need it.

Our charter of February 17, 1809, appears in the statutes as Seven Ohio Law 184, meaning the seventh year of Ohio statehood after 1803. It reads:

"*Section I.* Be it enacted by the general assembly of the state of Ohio, that there shall be an university established and instituted, in the manner hereafter directed, within that part of the country known by the name of the John Cleves Symmes' Purchase, [Symmes of New Jersey had put together the land company for the settlement of the area between the two rivers called Miami] which university shall be designated by the name and style of 'The Miami University' for the instruction of youth in all the various branches of the liberal arts and sciences, for the promotion of good education, virtue, religion, and morality, [these words are from the Northwest Ordinance of 1787, picked up and repeated in our charter of 1809] and for conferring all the literary honors granted in similar institutions; and the benefits and advantages of the said university shall be open to all the citizens within this state.

"*Section II Body Politic* Be it further enacted that the President and Trustees of The Miami University are hereby created a Body Politic incorporated by the name of 'the

President and Trustees of The Miami University,' which body politic shall consist of a president, and not more than fourteen or less then seven trustees whose time of service of appointment shall be for three years."

From the time of our charter, any legal action taken by Miami University is officially done in the name of "the President and Trustees of The Miami University." Any acquisition of property or sale of property, any bonds that are issued, are always in the corporate name. It is a Body Politic and the trustees are a governing board. The Board of Regents exists, but it does not dictate policy for Miami University, since it is for the purpose of coordinating, not of governing. The governing board of this university consists of the Board of Trustees together with the President, and it is stipulated in our charter that the trustees should be no less than seven, no more than fourteen in number.

When I became President in 1965, there were twenty-seven on the Board of Trustees. Our first woman chairman of the Board, Lucille Crowell Cooks, served for twenty-five years, and Paul McNamara, another chairman, served forty years, but there was one trustee who served fifty-five years, another fifty-two years, and still another fifty years. Thus the limit of three years in the original statute was many times changed, providing some advantage in stability, but also some disadvantage. It is difficult to change those who have been in positions of authority for most of a lifetime. Eventually, the State of Ohio stipulated that the Board of Trustees should have nine members serving terms of nine years and none could be repeated. The same rule applies for all the universities of the State of Ohio that are publicly supported.

The charter of The Miami University stipulated that The Miami University would be located in the area of the John Cleves Symmes Purchase. The problem was that the purchase was between the two Miami rivers, and by 1809 all the townships between the rivers had been settled.

There was no township within the limits of the Symmes Purchase which was unsettled and available to become a college township. Hence, it was agreed to set aside a college township outside the Symmes Purchase. This township, which would become Oxford, was located in the northwesternmost corner of Butler County, a county named for General Richard Butler who had lost his life in the Indian wars at the Battle of the Wabash, on November 4, 1791. Oxford Township is the home of Miami University, and the corner of it is still called College Corner.

The college township was supposed to support the university called Miami from the initial sale of lands and then from quit rents collected annually. Such rents are still being collected annually, with a few residents paying at the Treasurer's window every February at the typical rate of a dollar for a lot. Many property owners in Oxford like myself took the option some years ago of paying $25 invested at 4% so that we could avoid the trip to the Treasurer's window every February. By investing $25, you are guaranteed that your rent will be paid to support the university, because all landowners in the college township are required by law to pay the quit rent. Miami collects $7500 a year from the college township, though its campus was not originally required to be inside it; all that was required was that this land would support the college wherever it was located.

There was an initial effort to locate the township inside the Miami Valleys. A three-member Commission called for in the charter was appointed to look over the whole of southwestern Ohio and find the best site for a campus. When the three-man Commission was appointed, it began to receive applications. The first to apply was Cincinnati, the first settlement in the Symmes Purchase, the oldest and the largest town with a population of 7500. It was going to be the principal city in the Miami Valleys and wanted to have a university associated with it; it had an advantage in size. Another application was received from Dayton, a city named for Jonathan Dayton from New Jersey, a former Congressman and delegate to the Constitutional Convention. There was an application from Middletown, half-way between Cincinnati and Dayton. And there was an application from Hamilton, the county seat of Butler County, named for Alexander Hamilton, founder of the Federalist Party and first Secretary of the Treasury. Hamilton had been a fort in the Indian wars and its first structure was Fort Hamilton, on the banks of the Great Miami River. These were only the more prominent applicants, since Yellow Springs thought itself well suited to be a college community, and so, too, did Lebanon, in the valley of the Little Miami River.

It was up to the three-member Commission to decide on the location of Miami University, and so it elected to take a look at all the applicants. They visited each of the communities which had applied, but when they got to Lebanon, they fell in love with the place. They voted to recommend Lebanon as the site of The Miami University. The town was in an attractive area, with a beautiful valley, and the town of Lebanon, through a principal citizen, Ichabod Corwin by name, offered forty acres to the new school, free of charge. The forty acres were just west of a brand new inn at Lebanon called the Golden Lamb. It was indeed a beautiful spot for a campus, and one of the commissioners was so enthused that he took a hunting knife out of his waistband and carved in the bark of a great oak tree MUV: Miami Uni Versity. Just west of the Golden Lamb in Lebanon is still a great place, but Miami University was not put in Lebanon; it was put in Oxford. Why?

Well, there were howls of protest from the other applicants, from Cincinnati, Dayton, Middletown, Hamilton,

Yellow Springs, all crying foul. They protested that if they had known a gift of land would cause the Commissioners to favor them, they would have made land available. The proposed gift from Lebanon was land owned by Ichabod Corwin, and we have today the Corwin Nixon Aquatic Center in our new Recreational Center. Corwin Nixon is a direct descendent of Ichabod Corwin, and he served for years in the Ohio General Assembly from Lebanon. So the Corwin family has continued to take an interest in Miami University even though it's not located in Lebanon.

All the howls of protest about the choice of Lebanon reached the ears of politicians in the General Assembly in Columbus, who promptly did what politicians are often wont to do with a hot potato. If they decided on Lebanon, they would make one community happy but make a host of others very unhappy. So they ignored the recommendation of the three-member Commission, on the pretext that one of the three committee members had been sick and unable to visit Lebanon in person. Though he had subsequently visited the place, had liked it and had affixed his signature on the recommendation, the General Assembly said it couldn't accept the recommendation because he had not been physically present the day of the official visit. They took the hot potato, the decision where the school should be located, and tossed it over to the Board of Trustees of the new Miami University.

The Board was directed now, by General Assembly action taken on February 6, 1810, to find the campus site within the college township. When the earlier Commission of the General Assembly looked at sites for a new university, they looked at the whole of southwestern Ohio. Now, the Board of Trustees was told, find a site in the six-mile-square college township which is to be called Oxford. It was up to the Board of Trustees to find the site of the campus of Miami and the town of Oxford, and they duly appointed a five-member committee, which, in the last week of March

1810, began to make its way through the valley of the principal stream in the college township, which the Indians had named the Talawanda. Anthony Wayne and early settlers had called it Four-Mile Creek, a tributary of the Great Miami, but Talawanda has a more romantic, poetic sound and the musical word of Indian origin means "cloudy water." It is a comparatively shallow stream, and whenever there is a hard rain the Talawanda rises and the water becomes brown through erosion. So, much of the time, the Talawanda is roiled up by rains and storms. The converse of cloudy is clear, and the Indian word for clear was Sandusky. Perhaps when the Indians examined the Sandusky River and gave it the name, it was clear, whereas when they got to the Talawanda, it was all roiled up and therefore cloudy.

But why was it called Four-Mile Creek? General Wayne, in his campaign of 1794 against the Miami Confederacy, made encampments one after another at intervals of four miles, seven miles, and twenty-one miles, naming the stream where he encamped for the distance of travel since his last encampment. So we have not only Four-Mile Creek, but Seven-Mile Creek and Twenty-One Mile Creek. Four-Mile Creek is several times longer than Twenty-One Mile Creek, but its name came not from its length but from the distance Anthony Wayne and his men had marched since their last encampment.

Both names remain, but Talawanda has been used most frequently. We have in Oxford today Talawanda Road, Talawanda Lane, and the Talawanda City Schools. Outside Oxford, signs on the bridges over the stream read Four-Mile Creek, and so the Butler County Engineers call it Four-Mile Creek, even though many Oxonians call it the Talawanda. In looking for a site in the Valley of the Talawanda, the five-man committee of the Miami Board of Trustees moved through thickets and canebrakes until they came to the solitary two-story log house of the only settler in the college township at that time. He was a man of Dutch descent, Zachariah DeWitt, a relative of the former New York Governor DeWitt Clinton, builder of the Erie Canal. Zachariah and his wife Elizabeth and their eight children lived in a two-story log house that still stands. It is the oldest building in the college township today, dating from 1804-1805. When the committee got to that cabin, they asked Zachariah his advice about where to establish the campus of a university. He told them on the rolling hillcrest to be seen west of his home. The five members of the Board committee walked up that hillcrest and chose the site of Miami University.

As a result of their choice, you go up town in Oxford, not down town: we've been going up town ever since. The Board determined that the campus of Miami University would be on the east side of the town of Oxford, which would be a mile-square town, laid out in the English fashion. If it was going to be called Oxford, it ought to look like Oxford. All the streets were on compass points, east, west, north, south, and were given the names of the trees of the forest, Beech, Oak, Willow, Sycamore, except for the central thoroughfare, which was to be called High Street just as in Oxford, England.

The Board went on to determine that the campus would be wholly to the east, the commercial area would be in the center, and the residences would be north, south, and west. It was an excellent decision, since some campuses, including another beautiful one, Ohio University, have no such plan, and you find two residence halls and then a gas station, two more halls and then a Dairy Queen. Miami's campus is integral, and so is the town of Oxford. The Board called for a botanical garden on campus, and today we have in its place the formal gardens. The Board wanted Miami to have a beautiful campus, recognizing that aesthetic surroundings offer an important dimension in learning. It's easier to learn in a place that's attractive than in a place that's unattractive, so the Board called for trees, green lawns, flowers, brooks, ponds, to make the campus beautiful so that it would be a place of learning. They insured from the beginning that Miami would have a beautiful campus, and we are the beneficiaries of their long-range planning.

CHAPTER IV

PRESIDENT BISHOP OPENS THE DOORS

The question is often asked, why did it take Miami University so long to get underway? It was chartered on February 17, 1809, but classes did not begin until the first day of November, 1824, fifteen years later. There were a number of reasons for the long delay. First of all, it took some time to find the exact site. The General Assembly, in the Act of Charter, had originally provided for a three-member Commission of the Assembly to find the site somewhere in the area of the Symmes Purchase in the Miami valleys, making the whole of southwestern Ohio eligible. The three-member Commission found a site it liked in Lebanon and recommended it, but the legislature refused to accept the recommendation. They refused because they were under a barrage of protests from disappointed applicants in Cincinnati, Dayton, Middletown, Hamilton, and Yellow Springs, all calling "foul" and saying if they had known an offer of free land was needed, they would have made the same offer Lebanon had made.

Ichabod Corwin had offered forty acres of land immediately west of the Golden Lamb as a site for the campus of Miami University and the three commissioners had found exactly what they were looking for, but because of the howls of protest, the legislature refused to act and referred the matter to the Board of Trustees of Miami University. But they ordered the Board to find the site in the northwesternmost township of Butler County, which was set aside as the college township, provision being made as early as the act of Congress on May 5, 1792, for an educational township somewhere in the Symmes Purchase area. This act of Congress was reconfirmed in March, 1803, two days after the State of Ohio came into the

Union. The original stipulation had said there would be a township to support a university, but there had been no requirement that the university had to be in the college township, meaning that it could be situated anywhere in the Miami valleys. But on February 6, 1810, the General Assembly said to the Board of Trustees of Miami, find the site for the college in the college township, and call the village in which it is located Oxford. They specified the township and the name; it was up to the five-member Board of Trustees Committee to find the site in the Valley of the Talawanda or Four-Mile Creek. The committee asked Zachariah DeWitt, who had built a two-story log house on the banks of the Talawanda in the winter of 1804-1805, to recommend a site, and he looked up at the rolling wooded hillcrest to the west of his two-story log house and said put it there.

Today, the oldest building on the Miami campus is that two-story log house of Zachariah DeWitt and his family. It's worth seeking out; you just follow the Marcum Trail behind the Marcum Conference Center down to the valley, or you can walk east along Highway 73 past the stables, over the bridge that spans the Talawanda, turn left into a cindered parking lot, and from there take a graveled driveway that leads along the stream about a quarter of a mile to the DeWitt log house. You can even see the DeWitt cabin from Highway 73 when the trees lose their leaves, and it's a good place to walk on a pleasant sunny afternoon in the fall.

It did take time to find the site, but thirteen months after the act of charter, it was finally found. The second obstacle to getting a college underway was determining how to pay for it, how to build the buildings, and how to hire a faculty. Though the state had chartered the University, it did not provide funds to operate it: not one dime was appropriated to get the university started. State appropriation of funds to run the university did not come until after the Civil War, when the New Miami rose out of the ashes of the Old Miami in 1885. We were chartered in 1809, but it was seventy-six years after the act of charter that we finally had our first appropriation from the State of Ohio. We were always a public university, but we were not in fact a publicly supported university. How could we finance the buildings for instruction and hire a faculty to do the instructing without funds to pay for them? There was only one way to do it, and that was for the university to do what private colleges do: go out and raise the money.

Miami did have one financial asset, the college township. It was not a very large tract of land in those days, only about 23,000 acres, but the Charter gave Miami the income from the sale of land in the college township of thirty-six square miles, plus annual quit rents paid by the purchasers. The Secretary of the Board of Trustees, a young man from Hamilton named James McBride, was given the responsibility of advertising the lands available in the college township. He had been appointed Secretary because he was the youngest member of the Board at twenty-three, and because his hand-writing was the best. You could read it. And so signs began to appear in James McBride's beautiful hand-writing throughout the forest surrounding Oxford. "Lands for sale: contact the Miami Board of Trustees." He gave his own Hamilton address to would-be purchasers of "in-lots" inside the town of Oxford, the old mile square, and "out-lots" outside of town in the other thirty-five square miles. Understandably, the price of the in-lots would be somewhat higher than the out-lots. We still have in the university vault some of those hand-lettered signs put out on the trees around Oxford by James McBride. Eventually, the university would realize $7500 annual income from the quit rent paid by those who bought land inside the college township.

We also have one of the titles given by the Treasurer's

Office of The Miami University to a farmer named Finkbine, whose descendants still live west of town. It is dated 1827, and it stipulates that Mr. Finkbine has received 108.93 acres (or almost 109 acres) on which he must pay an annual quit rent of $16.34. The title to the land says that he or his heirs must pay the sum of $16.34 each year for ninety-nine years, and that the terms of the lease are renewable forever. Thus the university started with a fixed annual income totaling $7500 for the entire township, money that would keep it solvent for awhile.

I mentioned that I became one of the leaseholders at a later date and used to take my dollar bill down to the Treasurer's window in Roudebush Hall. Mine was a small lot, about three-quarters of an acre, and $1.00 was my annual charge. Then a dozen years ago the university realized that it was spending $15,000 to collect $7500. It had to send out notices, make collections, hand out receipts, and keep books on all of the land-owners in the college township. So the university offered people like me the chance to bring in a single check for $25.00, which it would invest at 4% interest to bring in $1.00 each year from that time on. I jumped at the chance to complete my rent payments to Miami in one transaction, but there are some die-hards in the college township who continue to bring in their dollars every year. As for the university, it is still getting $7500 from the college township— enough to run the place in the early nineteenth century, but not enough today to pay the salary of a single instructor. It is there for ninety-nine years, forever renewable, but it is not a very good business deal, because it totally ignores inflation. More money was needed to get the college started, and much more to keep it going as the years went by.

And hence, on the 29th of August, 1810, the Miami University Board of Trustees hired its first staff member, a fund-raiser (we would call him a development officer today) to go out and seek money for the new college.

The fund-raiser was the Rev. John W. Browne from Paddys Run, Ohio, near Shandon, a village south of Oxford in Butler County. The Rev. Browne was a Methodist minister, the Board no doubt reasoning that if there was anyone who could extract hard-earned dollar bills from tight wallets, it was a Methodist minister. He would serve from late August 1810 till January 1812. The first chapter of *The Miami Years* is about this "Beggar on Horseback," as Walter Havighurst calls him, the Rev. Browne who boldly set out from Butler County heading east on a horse. The Trustees had hired him with the understanding that if he was successful in raising money, he might some day be known as the Father of Miami University.

Rev. Browne agreed to work on commission, and he took his job seriously enough to start at the top. He rode all the way to Washington and went to see President James Madison in the White House. Madison said no to Rev. Browne's request for support, because he was receiving all kinds of requests for funds, and the Vice President, whose name was Clinton, gave him the same answer. So he approached the senators and congressmen from Ohio, and with them he had greater success. But he realized that he might do even better by visiting academic communities away from the capital. He headed north from Washington to such college towns as Princeton, New Jersey, New Haven, Connecticut, and Cambridge, Massachusetts, soliciting help for a new college in the beech woods out in southwestern Ohio. And he met with some success, collecting a dollar bill, fifty cents, a dime, even occasionally five dollars. But he did better at collecting books, since some who couldn't give money could give books. Eventually, in addition to the funds he collected, he had been given some two hundred books.

The oldest books acquired for Miami are those

brought back by the Rev. John Browne, and some of them are in the King Library today. He also acquired some pieces of scientific apparatus, and even a keg of whitewash, since one potential donor told him, "When you put up a building out there, you're going to have to paint it. Here's a keg of whitewash. Good luck." As he collected the books, apparatus, and kegs, he sent them off on the next wagon heading west with the label "Oxford, Ohio." He didn't know how long it would take, but he was willing to send it as far as it might go, say as far west as Pittsburgh. Then somebody might be heading west of Pittsburgh and would take it further, until finally it would reach Oxford, Ohio. All told, he raised about $1,000 and acquired about 200 books, hardly what was hoped for when he was hired.

Tragically, John Browne's life as a fund-raiser was cut short. He did not die, as reported, by drowning in the waters of the Little Miami River in August of 1812, but actually fell into the Little Miami in January of that year. He was a preacher who supplemented what he earned raising money for Miami by preaching from time to time. He had accepted a preaching assignment in a community in the Little Miami valley, but when he tried to ford the Little Miami River in the dead of winter, his horse slipped its footing and sent Browne plunging into the stream. The temperature was well below freezing, and though he didn't drown, he died of hypothermia. He had no place nearby where he could dry off and change clothing, so he came to a tragic end.

Did he realize his dream of becoming known as the Father of Miami University? Hardly. But his name is remembered on our campus—not by Brown Road north of town, which doesn't have an "e" on the end of it, but by The John W. Browne Stables just east of town. The stables are an appropriate place to bear his name, for after all, he was the beggar on horseback. So if he did not become the father of the university, he might be called father of the stables.

John Browne had not raised a lot of money, nor had income from the college township generated much at first. Land sales were slow to reach the $7500 income Miami was hoping to rely on each year. All in all, it took time to find the site, it took time to get the money, and then a war intervened in the midst of it all. The school was chartered in 1809, and three years later the country was plunged into the War of 1812. It was another war with England, the old motherland, and it was fought in large measure on Ohio soil and in Ohio water. The most significant naval action in the War of 1812 was fought on Lake Erie, and today we call it the Battle of Lake Erie or the Battle of Put-in-Bay. It was won by Commodore Oliver Hazard Perry over the British Commodore Robert Barclay, and the famed dispatch from Perry to his Commander-in-Chief William Henry Harrison was short but memorable: "We have met the enemy and they are ours."

How did the War of 1812 affect Miami? The university was chartered in Ohio, and the war was fought in large measure in Ohio. The first Miami teacher came in 1811, not to teach college-level students but to prepare younger students for college. His name was James Maxwell Dorsey, and his name, along with that of James McBride, is remembered in the names of two of our residence halls, Dorsey and McBride. James Maxwell Dorsey, an easterner, had come to teach the children of the college town in the college township. To house his class, a school—called a Select School—had been built where King Library stands today. It was not a very large structure, only eighteen feet by thirty feet, a single-story log building. Dorsey's instruction began in the fall of 1811 and continued in the spring of 1812, preparing prospective college students for the day the college would open. In the early history of America's colleges, the presence of an academy or preparatory school on or near the college campus was routine. The practice has not entirely ended, because when Xavier University in nearby Cincinnati celebrated its sesquicentennial, St. Xavier High School celebrated its sesquicentennial, too. St. Xavier High had been installed as the preparatory school for Xavier University. So Miami had a select school before it had a university, preparing students for college by teaching them some Latin, some Greek, and some Hebrew, the necessary pre-requisites for college entry.

This select school operated for one year, and then it was closed because of the War of 1812. Schoolmaster Dorsey went off to take charge of a Butler County regiment, being promoted to Major Dorsey so that he could command the regiment in its battle against the British. All education on the Miami campus came to a halt. The war lasted from 1812 to 1814; technically it was over on Christmas Eve of 1814 with the Peace of Ghent in Belgium. But news traveled slowly in those days, and the word that the war was over didn't get back to this country until weeks later in 1815. The most significant land battle in the War of 1812 ended with the victory of Andrew Jackson in the Battle of New Orleans, which was fought weeks after the war was over. Jackson didn't know it was over; the British didn't know it was over, and they fought as though the war was still going on. When the war did really come to an end in 1815, Major Dorsey was mustered out of the service and returned to the campus.

The Trustees were ready with a much larger responsibility than teaching preparatory classes. They converted the teacher into an architect to design the first campus building. He started in 1816 to oversee a building on the site of the present Harrison Hall, the west section of the main campus building. While that was underway, a second section was commenced in 1820, which was a center section. The building you see on the site today is not the old Harrison. For years the old building was referred to affectionately by Miami students as Old Main. It had been named Franklin Hall in honor of Benjamin Franklin, but all the students called it Old Main. In 1931, it was given a new name, Harrison Hall. Old Harrison lasted until 1958, when the last remnant of the original campus building was torn down, giving way in 1959 to the new Harrison Hall. The old western section had only lasted until 1867, but the center section remained standing until 1958.

With its first building under construction, still another obstacle arose to delay Miami's opening. A challenge came from the city to the south, Cincinnati, which had originally wanted to be the site of Miami University. Its application had been rebuffed, but it had become the largest community in the Ohio Valley with a population of some 7500 (roughly, the population of Oxford today without its students), and so, in 1814, it sought once more to get Miami out of Oxford before its first building was finished. Cincinnati started a college of its own, a private liberal arts college with some municipal support for a medical school. But a new Cincinnati Medical College was also underway, and so Cincinnati raised the cry to get Miami out of the beech woods in Oxford and down in Cincinnati, arguing that instead of two colleges, there should be one, and it would become The Miami University in Cincinnati.

In 1822, a bill was introduced in the General Assembly calling for just such an action: Miami University was to be located in Cincinnati, and the building underway in Oxford was to be used only for preparatory purposes as a subcollege. A fight was mustered to save Miami for Oxford, a fight led by two men in particular, James McBride and Joel Collins. McBride was the Secretary of the Board of Trustees and Collins was the Treasurer. Collins had long resided in Oxford near what used to be called Collins Run; it is today called Bull Run, a small stream that runs beside the present Peffer Park south of Oxford. Collins and McBride took the fight to the

General Assembly to keep Miami in Oxford, rejecting the arguments from Cincinnati that advantages of size, wealth, and culture could not be matched in an isolated spot in the woods. McBride and Collins shrewdly argued that Cincinnati was already too large, since all the vices known to mankind were to be found there. They countered that it would be best to keep young men in Oxford, where Miami students would enjoy an environment that was pure, undefiled, and uncorrupted. They extolled the advantages of having a college in a remote location, where young men would not be tempted by all the sins found in a city the size of Cincinnati. The General Assembly agreed that the new university should stay in the beech woods, but the fight with Cincinnati had caused another delay. Only after the bill was defeated could the Miami Trustees give the word to proceed with finishing the building, and only then could the university begin to recruit its first students. Thus, the choice of a site, the problems of funding a new university, the necessity of fighting the War of 1812, and the attacks from Cincinnati delayed Miami's opening for fifteen years after its charter was issued.

Finally, however, in early 1824, the first building was finished. At last, in the fall of 1824, Miami University could begin to offer classes. All that was needed was to find the leader who could guide the new university through its opening period. On the Miami Board was a man named David McDill, a graduate of Transylvania College in Lexington, Kentucky, and he knew just the man for the position. It was his old mentor, Professor Robert Hamilton Bishop, who, of all the instructors he had at Transylvania, had made the deepest impression upon him. Though there were other applicants and other potential candidates, the Trustees ultimately agreed with McDill and on July 6, 1824, voted to tender the presidency of Miami University to Robert Bishop. Bishop said he was interested, but he asked if there would be a suitable residence for himself, his wife, and their eight children. The Trustees promised to have a presidential mansion waiting for him. The only building they could offer other than Old Main, the academic building, was the select school house, a one-room dwelling 18 feet wide by 30 feet long—a spare cottage for a man, a wife, and eight children. It was hardly the presidential mansion they had promised Robert Bishop, but they thought that with some hard work rooms could be added, a second floor built, and the whole place painted to make it look good. It satisfied Robert Bishop, who accepted the presidency and arrived on campus with his family on September 14, 1824.

On Saturday, September 14, 1996, on the Miami campus, the 172nd anniversary of the coming of the Bishops was celebrated in a ceremony in the formal gardens where President and Mrs. Bishop lie buried today. Stones from Scotland were brought by faculty, staff, students, and alumni—twenty in all, the last one placed in position by Dr. Jonathan Bishop, the great-great-grandson of Robert Hamilton Bishop, who with eleven other members of the Bishop family made the trip for the ceremony in what is called the Circle of Remembrance. Dr. Jonathan Bishop came all the way from Minneapolis, Minnesota, to put in place near his ancestor's grave a stone from West Cult, the Bishop family farm in Whitburn, Scotland, a half-dozen miles from Edinburgh.

Robert Hamilton Bishop did not have an earned but an honorary degree from Princeton, though at Miami he has always been referred to as Dr. Bishop. He was born on July 17, 1777, in West Cult, a Scottish farming community (Cult means cultivator), on a thirty-acre farm owned and operated by William Bishop, his father, and Margaret Hamilton Bishop, his mother. They gave him his maternal grandfather's name of Robert Hamilton (Bishop). His parents hoped that someday he would enter the Presbyterian ministry, and for that purpose they sent him to the University of Edinburgh where he graduated in 1797, then on to the Selkirk Divinity School nearby. In 1802, having completed his divinity degree, he accepted a call from the Presbyterian Church in the United States of America and crossed the ocean to New York City, taking with him his wife, Ann Ireland, who had been his sweetheart for many years before they married. In September, 1802, they boarded a sailing ship from Edinburgh to cross the Atlantic to New York City, and there they got their assignment. They were to head west to the Ohio valley and be assigned to the Presbytery of Kentucky. Ohio was not yet a state, but Kentucky was already in the Union. Rev. Bishop's assignment was to do missionary work on both sides of the Ohio River.

Robert and Ann Bishop reached Ohio from New York, and arrived in Chillicothe in November, 1802, just as delegates were putting together the first Constitution for the proposed new State of Ohio. The Bishops saw the Ohio Valley for the first time in November, not the best time to come, yet they fell in love with the place. Dr. Bishop would say there was no more beautiful place in the world than the Ohio valley, and he meant it. In the winter of 1802-03, he would serve a couple of small churches in Adams County, Ohio, before Ohio entered the Union in March, 1803. Then in 1804 he took a position in Lexington, Kentucky, teaching during the week at the oldest school west of the Alleghenies, Transylvania College, and continuing to preach on the weekends. He was appointed to the position of Professor of Moral Philosophy at Transylvania, and would serve there for twenty years, from 1804-1824, during which time he would advance to the position of Vice President as well as Professor of Moral Philosophy. In those twenty years of service he would have many outstanding students, including Albert Sidney Johnston, ultimately a general in the service of the Confederacy, Senator John Breckenridge from Kentucky, Stephen

Austin, founding President of the Lone Star Republic of Texas, and Jefferson Davis, the only President of the Confederate States of America. One of his students was David McDill, who became a member of the Miami Board of Trustees. Virtually all who had him as a teacher regarded him as the best at Transylvania.

But by the early 1820s Dr. Bishop's experience at Transylvania was beginning to sour. He and President Horace Holley were no longer getting along well. They had some doctrinal differences within the Presbyterian faith, but the biggest difference between them was a philosophic difference over the rightness or wrongness of slavery. Holley was willing to accept slavery and states' rights, whereas Bishop was not. Bishop, in fact, favored abolition. The primary reason why Bishop was ready to leave Kentucky in 1824 was that Kentucky was a slave state, and he would come to Ohio to be President of Miami because Ohio was a free state. Under the Northwest Ordinance of 1787, the Ohio River was the boundary between slavery to the south and free soil to the north. Miami was thirty-seven miles north of the Ohio on free soil, and Bishop in 1824 was ready to make the move.

Dr. Bishop accepted the challenge of serving as Miami's first President, and soon hired a faculty to help him. He would be a full-time faculty member as well as President, teaching the subject he had taught so well at Transylvania, Moral Philosophy. To join him on the faculty, he appointed in the fall of 1824 John Annan, Professor of Mathematics, from Dickinson College in eastern Pennsylvania, and William Sparrow, a graduate of Trinity College in Dublin, Ireland. Thus Miami's first faculty included two out of three who were products of British universities, the University of Edinburgh in Scotland, and Trinity College in Ireland. The classical curriculum which they had mastered would be embodied in the first curriculum at Miami.

Finally, in the fall of 1824, the faculty was assembled and the president had been chosen for the new Miami University. It was time to advertise for students, and ads filled the papers in the fall of 1824 to indicate that the academic year would begin on November 1 and end on August 1 of the following year. The typical academic year at American colleges at that time was geared to the farm economy, since most of the students were farm boys. In November, the harvest was in and you could be released from your farm chores. The following August, you would be needed again on the farm to bring in the harvest. For the academic year at Miami in 1824-25, the advertisement called for $93.00 to cover all expenses. $50 was needed to cover your board—all your meals—since there were no residence halls at this point and no dining rooms, and students boarded with families in the community, who agreed to charge $1.25 a week for a forty-week year, or $50 to cover all meals. A room in town would cost $5.00 for the year, with the understanding that you would secure the services of someone who would be sure your room was clean and your bed was made. $8.00 for the year was to be allowed for washing, and $5.00 for candles and wood. Wood was the fuel everyone used, because there was no central heating, and each room had its own fireplace. You had to provide your own wood for keeping warm in the winter. Tuition at the university would be $20.00, with an allowance of $5.00 for incidentals for the entire year. So $93.00 was the grand total for the first academic year at Miami University. Obviously, there has been a bit of inflation since 1825.

The advertisements also announced the routine of the day at college, so that the prospective student would know what to expect when he got to Miami. The gist of the ads Dr. Bishop published in 1824 was this:

You can expect to arise at 5:00 in the morning when the bugle is blown for the first time. Then you will study from 5:00 to 7:00 a.m. At 7:00 a.m. you will have your first recitation, your first class. At the end of that hour, at 8:00 a.m., you will break your fast, that is, you will have breakfast. After breakfast, you shall assemble for morning prayers in the chapel on the second floor of the main academic building. Following morning prayers, there will be three hours of recitation, from 9:00 to 12:00; from 12:00 to 1:00 will be lunch; from 1:00 to 2:00 will be re-creation. You will allow three hours from 2:00 to 5:00 p.m. for study and preparation for the next day's recitations; from 5:00 to 6:00 p.m. you will have your evening meal; from 6:00 to 8:00 p.m. you will engage in more study [though if you have had sufficient study, you are allowed more re-creation]. At 8:00 p.m., you will assemble again for evening prayers. [Can you imagine the faculty and students praying together twice a day?] From 8:00 to 9:00 p.m. there would be a final hour of study; at 9:00 p.m. the bugle would blow, at which time all candles would be snuffed. Darkness would descend across the Miami campus and across the town of Oxford until 5:00 the next morning when the bugle would blow again, summoning you to the next day's events.

I go through this routine in some detail only because I occasionally hear from students about how mistreated they are, how they are chafing under all the restrictions and restraints, and I say all you need to do is review what was expected of Miami students in 1824, and indeed, for many years thereafter. Actually, there are fewer restrictions, fewer restraints on students today than at any time in the history of higher education.

The ads for the new university were placed, and the student body assembled. On November 1, 1824, there were twenty students who met the president and the faculty in the chapel for the beginning of the school year. Twenty. Of these, four were juniors, three were sophomores, five were freshmen, and eight were pre-college or preparatory students. Where did the five upperclassmen come from? Most were from Transylvania in Lexington. They had followed their old mentor Professor Bishop from Kentucky up to Ohio. It took Miami fifteen years to get going, but the first graduating class finished in two years because there were five juniors. And when they graduated in 1826, they would have on their diplomas a seal devised by Dr. Bishop and the first faculty, one of whom had already left.

Professor Sparrow had left Miami after only a year to become Vice President of the first church college in Ohio, located in Knox County. It was Kenyon College, founded by the first Episcopal Bishop of Ohio, Philander Chase, who was given 30,000 pounds of English currency, money enough to start a college quickly. The 30,000 pounds of English currency came from two men who had been the British representatives at the Peace of Ghent on Christmas Eve, 1814, which brought the War of 1812 to a close. A letter of introduction accompanied Bishop Chase across the Atlantic Ocean to contact Lords Kenyon and Gambier, who had been the British Commissioners at the end of the War of 1812. Henry Clay, the American representative at the peace talks, had prevailed on his old associates to contribute to the new school in Ohio, and in gratitude to them Bishop Chase named the college Kenyon and located it in a town called Gambier. Its athletic teams are appropriately nicknamed the Lords, and as far as I know, without a single protest. Professor Sparrow left Miami to become Vice President at Kenyon in 1825, and his place was taken by Williams Holmes McGuffey, who with Professor Annan and President Bishop would in 1826 devise our first Miami seal, the seal we still use on our diplomas to this day.

Chapter V

WILLIAM HOLMES MCGUFFEY, SCHOOLMASTER TO THE NATION

Classes began at Miami on November 1, 1824, with a faculty of three and a student body of twenty. The three members of the faculty included the President, Robert Hamilton Bishop, Scottish by birth and a graduate of the University of Edinburgh, who came to Miami from Transylvania College in Lexington, Kentucky. His field was moral philosophy, in which he instructed students at Transylvania for twenty years before coming to Miami. In addition to Dr. Bishop, the faculty consisted of John Annan, Professor of Mathematics, who came from Dickinson College in eastern Pennsylvania, and William Sparrow, Professor of Ancient Languages and Literature and first University Librarian, who came from Trinity College, Dublin, Ireland. It's significant that of our three initial faculty members, two were graduates of British universities, one in Scotland, one in Ireland. It's also significant that the first student body included four juniors, three sophomores, five freshmen, and eight pre-college preparatory department students. They were not all freshmen; we began with some juniors and sophomores, most of whom followed Dr. Bishop from Transylvania to Miami University. Surprisingly, of the dozen students ready for college classes, the ages ranged from twelve to twenty-one. But in those days, if you could pass the Latin examinations, you were in, even if you were twelve. If you couldn't pass them, you weren't in, and when you learned enough Latin to pass them, you were somewhat older at the start of your college career.

As noted before, in the advertisements that circulated through the newspapers of the Ohio Valley in 1824, indications were given to the students about what sort of regimen they would be expected to follow when they came to campus. The regimen began with the blowing of a bugle. Dr. Bishop hated bells, but he loved the clarion notes of the bugle. If he came back to the Miami campus today and heard all the bells—the Beta Bells on the main campus, the Heath Chimes on the Western College campus, the bells in many academic buildings—what would he think? He felt the bugle was the proper way to summon faculty and students to the regimen of the day, beginning at 5:00 in the morning when the notes of the bugle would rouse students from their slumber, calling them to two hours of study followed by an hour of recitation, after which they had breakfast. Afterward came morning prayers, followed by three hours of recitations—not lectures but interaction between professors and students, questions and answers about Greek, Latin, and Math—and then lunch, and "re-creation," as Dr. Bishop called it (we would call it "recreation"). Re-creation meant getting your energy back for an hour after lunch, followed by three more hours of study, then dinner, then additional study time, and then evening prayers. All faculty and students were expected to meet for both morning prayers and evening prayers. No one worried then about constitutional rights. The Constitution stated that Congress shall make no law respecting the establishment of religion or prohibiting the free exercise thereof. In the eyes of faculty on this campus and elsewhere, the Constitution did not forbid prayer, and you were expected to meet twice a day for prayer even on a public campus. After evening prayers, there was time for one more hour of study before the 9:00 bugle would blow and, as Dr. Bishop put it, all candles were to be snuffed. At 9:00, darkness descended on the Miami campus until 5:00 the next morning, when the bugle would blow to start the day all over again. Eight hours of sleep and then up and at 'em.

The old academic year began on November 1 and

ended on August 1, that is, it ran from the end of harvest to the beginning of harvest. Practically all of the students came to college from farms, and it was vital to the success of their families to get the crops in. You had from August 1 to November 1 to bring in the harvest, and on November 1 you were back in college. Cost for the entire academic year, including board, room, tuition, fees, laundry, and incidentals was a mere $93.00. Because there were juniors in the initial Miami student body, the first Miami commencement was in 1826. So, though it took fifteen years after the charter to get started, it took only two years to graduate the first class. Of course, the first class to graduate consisted of what we would call "transfer students," most of whom had accompanied Dr. Bishop to Miami from Transylvania in 1824.

For official certification that you had completed the degree of Bachelor of Arts, which all the early graduates earned, it was necessary to have an official seal and motto. In 1826, Dr. Bishop convened his small faculty to agree on the seal and motto. One faculty member of the original three had already left, because William Sparrow, Professor of Ancient Languages and Literature and Librarian, had, in 1825, accepted appointment as Vice President of the first church-related college in Ohio, Kenyon College at Gambier, the consequence of which was that President Bishop had to find his successor. He traveled far and wide to find the right person, but found him at last in Paris, Kentucky, in a one-room country school that had earlier been used as a smokehouse for the curing of hams, no doubt still smelling of smoke. The right person turned out to be William Holmes McGuffey.

And so it was that William Holmes McGuffey, along with John Annan and President Bishop, agreed in 1826 on a seal for the first diplomas, and that seal is still the official seal of Miami University, appearing on every diploma that has been issued since. There had been an original seal, to be sure, in 1810 when the first legal documents were processed, principally used for land sales and quit rents. That first university seal had simply shown a professor on one side of the desk and two students on the other side, in chairs. The new seal, in 1826, the one that is now emblazoned on ties, tie-tacs, notebooks, book covers, sweatshirts, and last but not least diplomas, shows three elements in a circle: an open book, a globe of the earth, and a telescope. These three elements symbolize the past, the present, the future. The past, represented by the open book, is the accumulated wisdom of the centuries which is passed to the present generation through their reading: note that the book is open, not closed, because only when books are open can they be read, and thus can impart to new minds lessons out of the past. As the book represents the past, the globe of the earth represents the present, signifying that people who live in various continents, countries, and cultures of the earth need to know about the rest of the world. The telescope represents the future, man's continuing quest to find meaning in the universe. Why are we here, on this particular planet, amid a galaxy of other planets and stars? The telescope is used to scan the universe and push back the frontiers of knowledge. With the circle of three elements are three Latin words: Prodesse Quam Conspici. These words are the Miami motto, the English equivalent of which is "to accomplish without being conspicuous." The key to life is achievement, not boasting about it; we are known by what we do rather than what we claim. The Miami seal appeared on the initial diplomas issued at the commencement in 1826, on a real sheepskin, and it has appeared on all diplomas since, most of them printed on heavy paper.

In the year 1828, President Robert Hamilton Bishop said he had a vision for the university over which he presided, and his vision was that someday it would become the Yale of the West. Though he was a product of an old

British university, a New England university had commanded his respect, and he declared that Miami should pattern itself after Yale. In the years that followed, the Yale image would come to be stamped on Miami in matters of curriculum, academic standards, and architecture. Dr. Bishop had arrived after the first academic building at Miami had been finished; it was officially called Franklin Hall, but was known to Miami students as Old Main. He was on campus, however, for the construction of our first two residence halls, called North and South Hall originally, but later named Elliott and Stoddard as we call them today. Both were consciously patterned after the oldest Yale building, Connecticut Hall, which dates back to 1756.

Dr. Bishop wanted the Miami campus to look like Yale's, and he also wanted faculty from Yale. A key appointment was that of John Witherspoon Scott, a Yale graduate, who came as the first Miami Professor of Science. As Professor of Science he taught all the sciences: chemistry, physics, biology, and geology. He and his wife built a home on the corner of Campus and High where, in 1832, a daughter Caroline was born. Caroline was destined to become the First Lady of the land, as the wife of the twenty-third President of the United States, Benjamin Harrison, a graduate of the Miami class of 1852. Today, the Phi Delta Theta National Headquarters stands on the site of the old Scott house. In the shrubbery at the corner of Campus and High, there is a boulder with a bronze tablet, which announces that it was on this site that Caroline Scott Harrison was born in 1832. Of all the faculty who served the university in the 1820s and '30s, John Witherspoon Scott was the closest friend of President Bishop. The two men saw eye-to-eye on nearly everything, as was not always the case with William Holmes McGuffey.

McGuffey had been hired by President Bishop to teach the ancient languages of Greek and Latin and serve as librarian, all of which he did very ably, but he coveted the class Bishop himself taught in moral philosophy. Ultimately, Bishop would stand aside and permit McGuffey to take his classes, but this generous action didn't entirely satisfy McGuffey. On many issues brought before the faculty, Scott and Bishop would be on one side, and McGuffey would be on the other. Yet despite their differences, Bishop recognized that McGuffey was exceptional, and he was right. Of more than five thousand faculty at Miami from the 1820s to the present, none ever reached the national acclaim of William Holmes McGuffey, who came to be called "Schoolmaster To The Nation."

McGuffey had come to Miami as a replacement for Professor Sparrow. William Holmes McGuffey arrived in 1826, riding behind his brother, Alexander Hamilton McGuffey, on a single horse. He was bringing his younger brother, Alex, to Miami to enroll him in the preparatory department. Though McGuffey was a bachelor when he came, he didn't remain a bachelor for long. He soon met Harriet Spining, the sister of an uptown merchant named Charles Spining, whose business was on the site of the old Miami-Western theater, now the First Run restaurant. Harriet Spining and William McGuffey met in 1827, fell in love and were married. They set up housekeeping in the only brick house then standing in Oxford on South Main Street. However, in 1828, a property became available on Spring Street not far distant from the main academic building and McGuffey's office, and they bought it. It was a frame dwelling when they bought it, but in 1833 they built a six-room brick addition. Though the frame house is long gone, the brick addition still stands, and today it is called the McGuffey House.

In that house, between 1834 and 1836, the first edition of the most celebrated textbooks in the history of this country were put together, widely known as the McGuffey Readers. They were compiled on a little eight-sided desk,

McGuffey's famous octagonal desk. It is like a lazy susan, the handy rotating table used in many families as a way of passing dishes around by simply turning the table top about a central pedestal. The octagonal desk of William Holmes McGuffey was built especially for him in 1834 by a local carpenter, enabling him to sit in his chair and turn from lesson to lesson, using the eight sides for eight different lessons. Each of the eight sides had its own drawer. You could sit in one position and your work would pass in front of you. It was an ingenious invention, exhibited for many years in the Miami library and now to be seen in the McGuffey House. McGuffey left Miami for Virginia in 1836, but his house and his desk are still on display in Oxford.

And, remarkably enough, the McGuffey Readers that he composed at that desk are still in print, and they have surpassed in publication all other books except the Holy Bible. The first edition came out in 1836, and more than a century and a half later, copies are still being sold. Though Margaret Mitchell's *Gone with the Wind* has been a bestseller for many years, and it has been said that its 28 million copies make it second only to the Bible, the McGuffey Readers have passed 130 million copies and are still being published. No school books in the history of the nation have had the impact of the McGuffey Readers.

When Walter Havighurst was asked in 1976 to give the bicentennial lecture commemorating the Declaration of Independence at the village hall in Oxford, he began by asking where the United States of America was born, and he answered that it was born in summer heat in Philadelphia, in winter snow at Valley Forge, and in a little house on Spring Street in Oxford, Ohio, where the most famed American school books were written. *The New England Primer* was the best known school book before the McGuffey Readers, but from 1690 when it was first published until McGuffey published his readers in the 1830's, only 5 million copies had been published, meaning that this book was never as influential as the McGuffey Readers.

Walter Havighurst pointed out that *The New England Primer* taught the alphabet beginning with "A is for Adam," and beside it was a somber couplet, "In Adam's fall, we sinned all." At the other end of the alphabet, the letter X was used to accompany a gloomy lesson about Xerxes, the warrior king of ancient Persia: "Xerxes the Great did die, and so must you and I." The New England primer was filled with death and dreariness, reflecting a period when the average age at the time of death was thirty. The here and the now was regarded as dismal and *The New England Primer* implied that life after death was our only hope: put up with the agony of the present in order to reach the paradise yet to come. That was Puritan Boston in the seventeenth century, but on the Ohio Frontier in the nineteenth century, Walter Havighurst remarked, McGuffey took a different approach to life, and of all the fifteen sets of school readers published between 1830 and 1841, the McGuffey series was by far the most popular. By the end of the nineteenth century, 100 million copies had been published, and the figure has passed 130 million by now. Why did the McGuffey Readers become the favorite American school books? Well, said Walter Havighurst, the first lesson in the first reader is "A is for ax." At that time, the ax was clearing roads and fields, building barns, dwellings, churches, school houses. On the frontier, everything was done by individuals, not by organized society, and the ax was a one-man implement. Walt Whitman in his poetry called it the homely weapon of democracy. And after ax in McGuffey's First Reader came other everyday things: box, cart, ox, vine, yoke. Instead of looking into a graveyard, McGuffey looked into the brightness of a new morning. A first grader was shown coming home from school with a poem on the sunrise:

The lark is up to meet the morn
The bee is on the wing
The ant its labors has begun
The woods with music ring.

McGuffey caught the spirit of the new nation, not weighed down with death but bursting with life and eager to build the future. McGuffey believed in the hereafter, since he was a clergyman as well as an educator. He was ordained a minister in Millville, Ohio, at the old Bethel Presbyterian Church in 1829. On Sundays, he preached at a church in Darrtown. He believed in the hereafter, but he also believed in the here and now, and in making the most of it. To him, the world was bright and green, not a dark world of misery and death. McGuffey's Readers were full of American optimism, preparing students to meet any challenge. They implied that one should look forward to the hereafter but also look forward to the years here on earth.

On April 20, 1833, William Holmes McGuffey entered into a contract with Truman and Smith, a publisher in Cincinnati, Ohio, agreeing to prepare a series of graded readers that would be eclectic in nature, meaning that they would comprise selections from a host of sources to which proper attribution would be made. The contract called for him to have $1,000 to start with, and if the book sold well, he would receive a ham every Christmas as a bonus. He signed the contract, and it was all he would get. He would make half a dozen publishers wealthy over the course of the next century and a half, but his total reward was $1,000 and a ham every Christmas. Of course, he had enormous satisfaction from the impact his books had in shaping the American character.

McGuffey subscribed to a new European educational

doctrine that was gaining currency in the nineteenth century, which held that whatever influences the life of a community or nation comes first through its schools. In order to make his readers responsive to children, he made the porch of his house on Spring Street the first laboratory school. He would bring neighborhood youngsters to his porch and try his lessons out on them; if they reacted favorably, he would keep them, but if they reacted unfavorably, he would change them or scrap them. McGuffey wanted each lesson to appeal to young children at the levels represented by his graded readers. He also wanted each lesson to incorporate a moral, because he believed that it was as important to teach children how to behave properly, and how to distinguish between right and wrong, as it was to teach them how to read and write and spell.

In recent years, there has been new interest in the McGuffey Readers, because some educators have advocated a return to moral values in education, noting that for some decades such values have been taken out of the American classroom. Though other educators have objected that our job is to teach students how to think, not how to behave, it has been argued that the reason our nation is the most crime-ridden among the major nations of the world is that we are producing intelligent crooks who are taught how to think but not how to behave. McGuffey believed it was important to teach both how to think and how to behave, and so every lesson had a moral.

One of the first McGuffey Readers shows two students sitting side by side in a warm classroom. One student looks over and sees a straight pin in the sleeve of the other, and thinks to himself, I'd like to have that pin. It's only a pin. And so, he reaches over to slip the pin out of the shirt of his neighbor, who is dozing away on a hot afternoon, unaware that the first lad is taking the pin from his shirt. But then, all of a sudden, the conscience of the thief takes hold, and he says to himself, wait a minute; this isn't my pin; it's my neighbor's. He thinks that what he has done is wrong and so he slips the pin back into the sleeve of the fellow who sits beside him. McGuffey observes: Think of the importance of that decision; had he taken that pin and not returned it and not been detected, he would have committed a little theft. And where would he be years later, if he took the pin, and did not feel remorse?

There were other lessons to be learned from McGuffey's Readers. A father comes into the room all upset, and asks his son, "George, who cut down my cherry tree?" To which the young twelve-year-old lad replies, "Father, I cannot tell a lie. I did it with my little ax." The father clasps the little boy to his bosom and says, "George, you've just made me the proudest father in all the land. I would rather lose a thousand trees than have you tell a lie." McGuffey then says that the boy grew up to be the President of the Nation and the Father of his Country: his name was George Washington, the man who could not tell a lie.

There are other stories with a moral import in McGuffey's Readers. For instance, a shepherd is out in the hills, tending his flock of sheep, day after day, and is bored stiff watching the sheep eat grass. He had been told by the villagers that if a wolf ever came, he was to cry "Wolf!" and they would come out with their sticks and brooms and shovels and cause the wolf to flee. But the boy is bored, and decides one afternoon to cry "Wolf!" Out come the villagers with their brooms and their sticks and their shovels, but there's no wolf to be seen, and the boy laughs. The villagers, however, don't see it as a laughing matter. They go back to the village upset. A few weeks later, a wolf does come and falls upon the flock and begins to devour the favorite lamb of the shepherd. Now the boy cries loudly "Wolf! Wolf!" but no one comes. They've heard the cry before, and so the boy has to watch as the wolf kills and eats his favorite lamb. McGuffey ends this story with the observation that one should always tell the truth.

Or, for another example of McGuffey's moral tales: Seven quarreling sons argue about who will get what from their dying father's estate. Covetous neighbors are aware of the quarreling sons, and they begin to gaze enviously at the property, taking advantage of the sons' division to scavenge for valuables. The father is on his death bed, but he sees that unless the seven sons stop their quarreling, the whole property is going to be taken over by covetous neighbors. He calls the seven to his bedside, asking each one to bring a stick. When they do, he takes the seven sticks and ties them into a bundle. He then asks each of his sons to break the bundle if he can. Each son takes the bundle and tries hard to snap it. The sticks won't break, and after the seventh son has tried and failed, the father asks to have the bundle back. They hand it to him, he unties it, takes each of the sticks and snaps it; one by one, all seven are broken. Then he points to the broken stack of seven sticks and says, "See how easily each one can be broken? If you continue to quarrel with each other, you'll be broken one by one and lose everything. But if you stand together, nothing in the world can break you." McGuffey then concludes that a family must stay together if it is to be strong.

Still another of McGuffey's stories is about two brothers, who are asked by their mother to bring home a bucket of fresh water from the village well. She sends them off to school with an empty bucket. After school is out, the two boys start home. To make a pole for carrying the water, they break off a branch of a tree, then go to the well and draw the water into the bucket their mother has given them. They hang the bucket in the middle of the pole and start home, with the small boy in front, the big brother behind. As they walk along, the big brother thinks to himself, my little brother is facing ahead. He can't see what I'm about to do. I'll just jiggle the pole a little bit and the bucket will begin to slide down toward the shoulder of my little brother. He'll have the whole weight. The big brother begins to jiggle the pole and sure enough, the bucket slides down till the whole weight is on the shoulder of the little brother. The little brother feels the weight grow heavier and heavier, and wonders if he can carry it all the way home. He doesn't realize what his big brother has done. But the big brother begins to have qualms about what he has done, and thinks to himself that it is wrong. His conscience overtakes him. What does he do? He lowers his end and begins to jiggle the pole again, and sure enough, back down the pole comes the bucket. Now it's weighing on the shoulder of the big brother, and the little brother feels it is getting easier to carry the bucket. The big brother shoulders the heavier load and thinks he has done what's right. My brother is smaller, but he is my brother. And McGuffey adds as his moral that it's important for the strong to take care of the weak.

One of my favorites is a poem in the Third Reader. I liked it so much that I began to read it to my wife, thinking she had never heard it before. But half-way through my reading, she took over and finished it from memory, explaining to me that she had memorized it sixty-five years before. So here was proof that the McGuffey lessons stuck. The poem is entitled "Which Loved Best?"

I love you mother, said little John
Then forgetting work, his cap went on
And he was off to the garden swing
Leaving his mother the wood to bring.

I love you mother, said Rosie Nell
I love you better than tongue can tell
Then she teased and pouted for half the day
Till her mother rejoiced when she went to play.

I love you mother, said little Fran
Today I'll help you all I can.
How glad I am that school doesn't keep
So she rocked the baby till it fell asleep.

Then, stepping softly she took the broom
And swept the floor and dusted the room
Busy and happy all day was she
Helpful and cheerful as child could be.

I love you mother, again they said
Three little children going to bed.
How do you think that mother guessed
Which of them really loved her best?

McGuffey's lesson was that actions speak louder than words, and his Readers proved the point: they influenced five generations of Americans from the 1830s to the 1920s. His books went out of favor in the 1920s primarily because they were written for an earlier period when we were an agricultural, rural people. As we became increasingly urbanized and suburbanized, school children found it hard to understand the stories about pigs and cattle and chickens. When McGuffey's books went out of favor (in the 1920s), they were not replaced. When I checked recently with an Amish Mennonite school in eastern Holmes County, Ohio, in one of the poorest districts in the entire state, I found it had stood in the top ten percent in the state proficiency tests. Not surprisingly, when I checked to see what text books they were using, I found they weren't using American but Canadian books that were in the McGuffey tradition, incorporating moral precepts in their lessons. It may be that the time has come for another McGuffey, whose books will not be about the rural agricultural life of 160 years ago, but will appeal to the urban-suburban life of the present, yet will teach a moral with each lesson.

William Holmes McGuffey stayed at Miami until 1836, when he left to assume the presidency of Cincinnati College. From there he would shortly go to Ohio University at Athens as President, then on to the University of Virginia, where he finished the remainder of a distinguished career. McGuffey is buried in the University of Virginia cemetery in Charlottesville.

But the McGuffey tradition is still alive at Miami, since our laboratory school for years was the McGuffey School, and now we have a McGuffey Foundation School at the west end of town. When McGuffey served with Robert Hamilton Bishop, Miami had a pair of great educators, and in the 1830s the university came to be recognized as the pre-eminent college in the West. Of the fourteen colleges west of the Alleghenies in 1838, Miami was regarded as the best. It was also the fourth largest American college, trailing only Harvard, Yale, and Dartmouth.

But Bishop's days were numbered, as McGuffey's had been. Unhappily, in 1840, Bishop was fired by the Board of Trustees, who had listened to charges that he was too lax in student discipline and too tolerant of the secret societies that had emerged on campus in the form of Greek letter fraternities. The faculty would ultimately respond with a rule against secret societies in 1841, precipitating a decade of ill will on campus, sometimes referred to as the "sullen years," under Presidents George Junkin and Erasmus McMaster, the successors of Robert Hamilton Bishop.

CHAPTER VI

MOTHER OF FRATERNITIES

By the year 1838, just 14 years after it finally opened its doors, Miami University had become the fourth largest university in the nation, with an enrollment of 250 students, exceeded only by the enrollments at Harvard, Yale, and Dartmouth. Quantitatively, it had clearly grown to be prominent, and qualitatively, it had become equally prominent. Among the fourteen colleges and universities west of the Alleghenies, Miami had the highest academic reputation. President Bishop wanted Miami to be the Yale of the West, and by the late 1830s, he might have felt he had reached that goal. But sadly, it was then Dr. Bishop was asked to resign by the Board of Trustees.

There were in fact two terminal years for Dr. Bishop, 1840 and 1841, because he was asked to resign twice. The main issue was the new fraternity system that had taken over at Miami. First, in 1840, there was dissension among the faculty and the Board about student discipline, and Dr. Bishop was asked to leave because he was believed by some to have become too lax. But it was the issue of fraternities that prompted the Trustees to oust Dr. Bishop. Secret societies with secret rituals for their members had grown strong at Miami, the antithesis, many thought, of a free and open campus, and since Dr. Bishop defended the fraternities, some thought he had to go.

But though he was dismissed in 1840, his replacement refused to come, embarrassing the Trustees into asking Dr. Bishop to stay at Miami one more year after he had been fired. He stayed for an additional year as President, then returned to full-time faculty status for several years, and finally left Miami altogether to accept a position at Farmers College in Cincinnati. At the time President

Bishop was asked to resign, an anti-secret society resolution was being formulated which would be adopted in the administration of Bishop's successor, Dr. George D. Junkin. Approved by the Board of Trustees in the fall of 1841, the resolution read:

> Resolved that the faculty be requested to require every student of this institution who is known to be connected with a secret and invisible society to withdraw from it forthwith and that it is hereby declared to be unlawful for any student in the future to become a member.

Strangely, fifty years after the adoption of this anti-secret society resolution, Miami was known across the land as the "Mother of Fraternities." And a century later, one-sixth of all the members of the Greek fraternities and sororities in the United States and Canada would be connected with fraternities or sororities founded at Miami University; thus, it is not too much to say that the Greek fraternity system was founded at Miami University.

But Robert Hamilton Bishop was dismissed from the presidency of Miami mainly because of the growing fraternity influence, and his place was taken by George D. Junkin, who came from Lafayette College in eastern Pennsylvania, for what proved to be a brief term of service, a mere three years. President Junkin was short but solidly built, far more autocratic than President Bishop, and he was every inch the stern disciplinarian that the Trustees believed they needed at that time. He was a Presbyterian minister, as Dr. Bishop had been, but was regarded within the Presbyterian Church as "old school" in his theology, whereas Dr. Bishop tended toward the "new school" point of view. Junkin quickly announced in a chapel session his philosophy about leadership on a college campus, declaring that the best administration is monarchical, with the president serving as king. Faculty and students accustomed to the more moderate administration of President Bishop were unprepared to have a new president take the role of king. George Junkin's tenure as Miami monarch did not last long, and it was his administration which initiated what have been called the "sullen years" of Miami history. From 1841 to 1849, there was a definite malaise on campus, with the result that George Junkin stayed only three years before returning to Lafayette. From there, he would accept the position of President of Washington College in Lexington, Virginia, which after the Civil War appointed Robert E. Lee to the presidency and eventually renamed itself Washington and Lee.

Bishop, believing slavery wrong, had been persuaded to leave Kentucky for Ohio, but Junkin, as President of Miami, was an outspoken defender of slavery. He went so far as to defend the principle of slavery in an address given at Hamilton, the Butler County Seat. Later, he made his home in Virginia, moving to a key slave state in the Confederacy. There, in Lexington, one of his daughters fell in love with and married a young math instructor at a neighboring school, the Virginia Military Institute. Her husband was Professor Thomas Jackson, famous in the Civil War as "Stonewall" Jackson, Robert E. Lee's chief lieutenant in the Confederate Army. Appropriately, George Junkin lies buried today in the Stonewall Jackson Memorial Cemetery in Lexington, Virginia.

Recently, Miami received a communication from one of our alumni who had visited that cemetery and had taken down the inscription on Dr. Junkin's tombstone. He recorded the facts that the Reverend George Junkin, D.D., LL.D., son of Joseph Junkin and Eleanor Cochrane of Cumberland County, Pennsylvania, had been born November 1, 1790, and died May 20, 1868. The tombstone reported less factually that he was the founder of Lafayette College, Easton, Pa., and of Miami University,

Oxford, Ohio. The truth was that Junkin had been the second Miami president, not the first, and he didn't come on the scene until 1841. Yet his tombstone declares him to have been the founder of Miami University, and it goes on to say he was President of Washington College from 1846 to 1861. The last achievement is undisputed, but the claim that he was founder of Miami is refuted silently on this campus: we have no Junkin Hall, no Junkin Arch, no Junkin Garden, no Junkin, period. The three years under President Junkin were not a very happy experience.

His place was taken, in 1845, by one Erasmus McMaster, who came from Hanover College, on the Ohio River in southeastern Indiana. Hanover is a Presbyterian college, and McMaster was the third consecutive Presbyterian minister to head Miami University. Unlike George Junkin, Erasmus McMaster was opposed to slavery; in fact, he was a confirmed abolitionist. There was good reason for him to live on the north bank of the Ohio River in the free state of Indiana, opposite the slave state of Kentucky. In his opening remarks, President McMaster extolled the free soil of Butler County, Ohio, a positive sign for his presidency, but unfortunately, there were some negative signs as well, and they eventually undermined his leadership.

Tall, distinguished looking (these were not negatives), he had a long memory (not a negative either), except that he could not remember students' names or faces. It was said of him that he had memorized both Homer's *Iliad* and *Odyssey* and could repeat them from memory in either Greek or Latin. And yet, despite this profound memory, he could not recall the names and faces of a mere two hundred students on campus. He was also lacking in good judgment and common sense, for he was disposed, on occasion, to make disparaging remarks to the students, and even to suggest to some students in public that they ought not to have come to Miami. Worst of all, McMaster frowned on fraternities, and they knew it; some of their members brought him to grief when, in 1848, they staged what has become known as the Snowball Rebellion.

In his earliest months at Miami, Robert Hamilton Bishop had affirmed his strong belief that there was a need for small groups to be organized and active on campus. In Miami's first year, there were only twenty students, but in the second year, which began in November 1825, Miami had over one hundred students. Dr. Bishop felt that a student body of one hundred is too large to give every student the opportunity to develop to his maximum potential; he argued that every student needed to have the opportunity to debate important issues and to participate in the life of the university. He wanted to assure every student some kind of leadership role, and he felt that if there were many small groups, each with a president, vice president, secretary and treasurer, opportunities would multiply for students to mature as leaders. It was his view that the influence of the faculty of three at Miami could be greatly increased if student organizations came into being.

Thus, President Bishop, in the second year of Miami history, 1825-26, welcomed the first two organized groups on campus, the Erodelphian and Union literary societies. The Erodelphians were formed in November of 1825, the Unions in December of that same year. As their names suggest, these literary societies were created for the enrichment of moral and intellectual life on campus. Every student could belong to one or the other, and these first literary societies had their own rooms assigned to them. They could meet, keep records, even amass their own libraries. Within twenty years after they started, the libraries of the Erodelphian and Union literary societies exceeded the library of the university in combined number of volumes. Rooms were assigned to them on the third floor of the Old Main academic building, with the Erodelphians to the left and the Unions to the right. The

Erodelphians adopted the color red and the Unions adopted the color white, the two Miami school colors to this day. These literary societies would last for a hundred years, from the 1820s to the 1920s, before they finally gave way to the social fraternities. What they left behind were the school colors of red and white, books of minutes in our archives, and three Erodelphian graves in the university plot in the Oxford Cemetery—all reminders that at one time literary societies flourished on the Miami campus.

The literary societies were gradually replaced by the Greek letter fraternities, the first of which did not come to the campus until the decade of the 1830s. The first Greek fraternity, Alpha Delta Phi, came to Miami in 1833. It had been chartered in 1832, at Hamilton College in New York, but it was not the first college fraternity, since Phi Beta Kappa had started at William and Mary as early as 1776. Phi Beta Kappa had originally combined social and academic purposes, but eventually it would become an honor society and cease to be a social fraternity. Alpha Delta Phi, however, was a social fraternity, and when one of its members graduated from Hamilton College, he was hired by a law firm in Cincinnati headed by Salmon P. Chase, later Governor of the State of Ohio.

Samuel Eels was his name, and he joined the firm at about the same time a Miami graduate, William S. Groesbeck, was also hired. They became good friends, and as their friendship deepened, they began to compare notes about their experiences in college. Groesbeck talked about the literary society to which he had belonged at Miami, and Eels talked about the social fraternity to which he had belonged at Hamilton. Groesbeck came to believe that the Greek letter fraternity, Alpha Delta Phi, offered something more than the literary society, because Eels talked about brotherhood, about young men enjoying life together on a college campus through a fraternity.

Groesbeck concluded that he had missed something, and invited his good friends still at Miami, Charles Telford and John Temple, to meet Samuel Eels. Eels explained the brotherhood of Alpha Delta Phi to Telford and Temple, who decided they would like to be members, so Eels inducted them into membership in 1833. The two returned to Miami and formed a fraternal association, which had grown to nine members by 1835. They approached President Bishop one day and asked for his presidential blessing. Since Bishop continued to promote small groups on campus, he gave them his blessing in a chapel meeting in the Old Main academic building. Dr. Bishop publicly welcomed what he understood to be the society of Alpha Delta and Phi to the campus, giving it his stamp of approval and committing himself in 1835 to endorse college fraternities in principle.

But the advent of the first Greek letter chapter west of the Allegheny mountains led to an immediate estrangement between the literary societies and the new fraternity. The literary societies adopted defensive bylaws, stating that a student could not simultaneously be a member of the Erodelphian or Union society and a member of a fraternity. This hostile division remained for a number of years, until in 1839, the president of the Union Society, John Reily Knox, organized a second Greek chapter on this campus. It was the first Greek fraternity originating at Miami, and John Knox and his friends proposed to call it Beta Theta Pi.

Eight young men, including Knox, met on the 8th day of the 8th month of the year 1839, in a room in the main academic building, to form the charter of the new fraternity. The commemoration of that meeting appears in a bronze tablet on the first floor of Harrison Hall today. However, this second Greek chapter was not publicly welcomed, because President Bishop and his staunchest supporter, Professor John Witherspoon Scott, were already under attack from other members of the faculty and the trustees over their approval of the first group, Alpha Delta Phi. The members of the new Beta Theta Pi chose to become a sub-rosa group for a number of years, operating secretly but expanding their organization to include chapters on other campuses.

Within a year, Beta Theta Pi had colonized on the campus of Cincinnati College, which in 1870 became the University of Cincinnati. It expanded to the East Coast as well, establishing a chapter at Harvard, then at Princeton, then at the University of Michigan and at Indiana University. The Betas, as they came to be called, showed the ability to grow even while they remained subrosa, because the anti-secret society resolution was passed by the trustees in 1841 forcing them to remain a secret and underground society. Neither the Betas nor Alpha Delta Phi were recognized publicly until 1846, in the administration of President Erasmus McMaster.

The anti-secret society resolution had not been repealed, but McMaster would not rigorously enforce it, and so the President of Miami and the Greek fraternities stayed at a safe distance from each other. It was the misfortune of McMaster that his tacit disapproval of the fraternities would lead to the campus disruption of January, 1848, the event notorious in Miami history as the Snowball Rebellion.

It all began innocently enough on a Wednesday evening, the 12th day of January, 1848, when a dozen Miami students returned from uptown Oxford where they had attended a church prayer meeting—hardly a likely place for a rebellion to begin. It had been snowing while they were at the prayer meeting, and the campus was covered with a thick blanket of snow, white and fluffy and easy to pack into snowballs. They quickly started making snowballs and throwing them at each other, until someone had the bright idea of forming a larger snowball. They pushed it along the ground to make it grow, and it grew so large one student couldn't push it by himself, so another one joined him and then a third, and the snowball got larger and larger. They were coming down what they called the slanting walk, which is now called Slant Walk, and there in the evening dusk, they confronted Old Main. Old Main served as both the classroom and administrative building: there, President McMaster had his office; there, they met for compulsory chapel; there, they had all their classes. Quickly, they decided to push it toward Old Main. They pushed it up to the front door, then added another huge snowball and another, until the whole front door was blocked by an enormous pile of snow. Satisfied, they went back to their rooms in the North and South dormitories, the buildings we call today Elliott and Stoddard Halls.

The next morning, at 5 o'clock, the janitor arrived to warm the rooms up for classes and chapel. There was no heating plant on campus; rather, the buildings were heated by lighting fires in individual fireplaces. When the custodian arrived at 5:00 in the morning to light the fires and get the chill off the classrooms and the chapel, he found the front door blocked with a huge mountain of snow. The custodian saw the impasse and informed President McMaster about it. The President had long been critical of students who ought to be somewhere else than at college, and now he had good reason to condemn them.

When the snow was finally removed and the door opened, chapel was convened, if a bit belatedly, and President McMaster announced he was determined to get to the bottom of the incident. He said he would find out the name of every student that had anything to do with blocking the door, and he would see that they were all expelled from the university. The students knew they were facing disciplinary action, and decided they would as soon be hung for a sheep as for a lamb, and so the Miami students involved in the episode of Wednesday night, January

12, 1848, decided to do it again the following night on a larger scale. They told their fraternity brothers and friends that the next night they would really do a job on the main academic building. They were confident that President McMaster couldn't kick everybody out, but they didn't know McMaster.

The next night, Thursday, January 13, brought more snow, fresh snow which still packed easily. They were determined now not only to fill the lobby and some of the rooms with snow, but to reinforce the snow by using the entire winter fuel supply of the university, which consisted of many cords of cut wood. In their zeal to block the building for good, they embedded in the snow not only the entire fuel supply of the university but also countless chairs and benches and desks and tables. They even cut the bell out of the belfry on top of the building. (By this time, Dr. Bishop, the man who hated bells, was gone, and Miami had replaced the bugle with a bell.) After cutting the bell loose, they dropped it in the college cistern, and watched it fall with a splash many feet below. Then they proceeded to nail the windows shut and the door shut. As a final ingenious prank, they partially severed the bell rope, so that a yank on it would snap the rope in half, leaving no way to climb up above the snowline in the building. Having done a good night's work, far beyond what they had done the night before, the men of Miami returned to their rooms.

Next morning, the custodian arrived again to open the building, only to find it totally sealed, frozen shut, because during the night the temperature had plummeted and the wet, mushy snow had congealed into solid ice. It was hours before the custodian, the President, and the faculty could shovel their way to the door to open it, and there were no classes on Friday, the 14th of January. Further, there would be no chapel Saturday or Sunday, since they had to clear out the icy mess inside the building. On Monday, when there was clear access to the building at last, it was decided that instead of holding classes, they would hold court. The President convened the faculty as judge and jurors to investigate and to punish the students responsible for the outrage. But the students refused to name the culprits who had organized the rebellion. The result was two solid weeks of trial. And when a student would finally be compelled to admit his involvement and would be expelled, his brother students, having hired a brass band, would serenade the expellee and carry him out of the room and across the campus on their shoulders, a hero.

In the course of the proceedings, every Greek on campus was expelled. Every member of Alpha Delta Phi and of Beta Theta Pi was forced to leave—except for two senior Betas who were just months from graduation and had taken no part in the rebellion. They stayed through to commencement, but after their graduation, there would not be a single solitary Greek left at Miami. All had been kicked out, and some of the expelled fraternity men went to other campuses to found other chapters. At Center College in Kentucky, Betas expelled from Miami moved south and established a new Beta Theta Pi chapter on campus.

So Miami faced a gloomy spring and an even gloomier fall. In the new academic year of 1848-49, enrollment had plummeted to sixty-eight students. A decade earlier, Miami was the fourth largest college in the country, but now it was one of the smallest. The college might have come to an end, as that dreary fall dragged on to Christmas break. But only some of the students who lived near Oxford went home for Christmas, and the remainder stayed on campus, where in a student room on the second floor of the northeast hall (today called Elliott), Robert Morrison and five friends founded a new fraternity. It was the day after Christmas, December 26,

1848, when Morrison and his friends, over a bottle of melted snow water, capped and preserved since the rebellion of the preceding January, agreed solemnly to establish a new Miami fraternity they proposed to call Phi Delta Theta.

Thus, after only one term without a fraternity on campus, Miami had a new fraternity as of December 26, 1848. With so few Miami students left, President McMaster was soon dismissed by the trustees, mainly for his uncompromising rigidity in expelling the participants in the Snowball Rebellion. There was, at one time, a McMaster Hall on campus, but it was a World War II barracks that stood behind the present Withrow Court, and it came down in 1976 when the Goggin Ice Arena was built. Since then there has been no commemoration of Dr. McMaster, who left the Miami presidency at the end of the second semester of 1849.

As the new Miami president, the trustees appointed a theologian from Dayton, another Presbyterian minister by the name of William C. Anderson. He was the brother of Charles Anderson, a Miami graduate who later became Governor of the State of Ohio. A residence hall is named for William Anderson, who came to Miami in the fall of 1849, and happily brought an entirely new spirit and a new direction to the campus. He was determined to re-establish the bonds between students and faculty that had been strong under Dr. Bishop, and to bring an end to the animosity that had prevailed since the anti-secret society resolution had been adopted in 1841. In his five years as President, Miami enrollment steadily rose from its low point, only 68 students during the last year under McMaster, to 266 students, greater even than the highest enrollment under Dr. Bishop.

In extending the hand of friendship to the students, President Anderson did something that would have been unthinkable to Junkin or McMaster. He agreed to accept a membership bid from the new fraternity, Phi Delta Theta. Here was a tangible way to show that the days of antagonism were over; he not only accepted the bid but so did his son John, who was an undergraduate at Miami. The two Andersons, father and son, both became Phi Delts. Miami prospered under Anderson, a strong faculty was hired, and healing took place in the residence halls under the kindly gaze of Professor of Classics Charles Elliott and Professor of Science Orange Nash Stoddard.

Dr. Anderson's appointment of these two faculty members as hall residents was the predecessor by some eighty years of what today we would call the resident advisor system. Charles Elliott as resident in the north hall gave his name to Elliott Hall, while Professor Stoddard as resident in the south hall gave his name to Stoddard Hall. There was also a renewal of the earlier Miami fraternities, the Beta Theta Pis and the Alpha Delta Phis, both of which would re-establish the chapters that had been closed following the Snowball Rebellion.

There was even a fourth fraternity at Miami, a new chapter not previously on campus, when Delta Kappa Epsilon, following a split within the ranks of Phi Delta Theta over the age-old question about the consumption of alcohol, formed a new society in 1852. More than half the Phi Delts condemned the use of alcohol, led by David Swing who, in the course of the nineteenth century would emerge as the Billy Graham of the nation, one of our foremost liberal theologians and a Miami graduate of the class of 1852. He was joined by Benjamin Harrison, later elected the 23rd President of the United States, to form a majority within Phi Delta Theta opposed to alcohol. But a minority, led by Gideon McNutt, took the opposing view. McNutt and several others saw no reason to exclude alcohol from the social program. McNutt and his group were expelled from the Phi Delta Thetas, and following their expulsion, they met Jacob Cooper, a member of Delta

Kappa Epsilon and a student at Yale University, which had a fraternity system much like Miami's. Cooper persuaded McNutt and his associates to join the Dekes, with the agreement that they would never argue about the use of alcohol.

So in 1852, a Miami chapter of the Dekes was established with Gideon McNutt as its central figure. Curiously, three years later, the Dekes would split over an inconsequential issue, a political contest on campus for the position of Poet of the Erodelphians. It was no longer forbidden to be in a fraternity and in a literary society at the same time, but the Dekes split into two factions over the question of who should be the Erodelphian Poet. One of the factions was led by Whitelaw Reid, later to be founder, publisher, and editor of the *New York Tribune*, rivaling the *New York Times* for many decades as New York City's principal newspaper, and still later an Ambassador from the United States to England, and a candidate for Vice President of the United States in 1892. The other faction was led by Benjamin Piatt Runkle, who would also become a man of great distinction, a Civil War general and a well-known journalist. The Runkle faction broke away from the Dekes and in 1855 established Sigma Phi, which soon changed its name to Sigma Chi. Three of these Miami fraternities would become known as the Miami Triad: Beta Theta Pi, founded in 1839, Phi Delta Theta, founded in 1848, and Sigma Chi, founded in 1855.

One other fraternity was started at the Old Miami. In 1868, John McCurdy Robinson transferred from Western Reserve in Hudson. He was a member of Delta Upsilon, the first non-secret fraternity, which had been founded at Williams College in 1834, with James A. Garfield, himself a future President of the United States, as one of its founders. With the coming of DU to Miami in 1868, the Greek system was firmly in place, and Miami was on its way to becoming known as the Mother of Fraternities.

CHAPTER VII

"THE TERRIBLE SWIFT SWORD": MIAMI AND THE CIVIL WAR

The sullen years of the 1840s, during the administrations of George Junkin and Erasmus McMaster, gave way in 1849 to the happy years of William C. Anderson, who was President of Miami until 1854. Not only did Anderson encourage fraternities, but he brought to the campus some outstanding faculty members, among them Charles Elliott, Professor of Greek, and Orange Nash Stoddard, Professor of Science. Dr. Anderson had a remedy for student rebellion: close contact between faculty and students, with faculty living in the residence halls and serving as proctors. Professor Elliott was assigned the residence hall to the north, the one that had been built in 1828, while Professor Stoddard was assigned the residence hall to the south, the one completed in 1835; these residence halls are called Elliott and Stoddard to this day.

As his facility for the instruction of all science classes, Professor Stoddard had a building which was added to the campus in 1838 and affectionately called "Old Egypt." Though it housed all the scientific apparatus of Professor Stoddard, it later housed the Egyptian collection of a noted Egyptologist on the faculty, Dr. Henry S. Osborn, and it was for this reason that the students nicknamed it "Old Egypt."

In addition to Professors Elliott and Stoddard, another faculty member brought to the campus by William Anderson was the son of the first president, Robert Hamilton Bishop, Jr, later to be known as "Old Bobby." He was employed as Professor of Latin and served with distinction until his retirement in the 1880s. President Anderson also hired David Swing, a graduate of the Miami

Class of 1852, first as instructor in the preparatory department, then in Moral Philosophy. David Swing in the course of the nineteenth century would emerge as a leading preacher of that era, becoming identified as one of American's foremost theologians after he left Miami for a church in Chicago.

Elliott, Stoddard, Bishop, and Swing together comprised an outstanding faculty in the period of the 1850s. That same era witnessed a return of good feeling between the Miami administration under Dr. Anderson and the student body, evidenced by the coming of additional Greek letter chapters, and the strengthening of the faculty through the appointment of Elliott, Stoddard, Bishop, and Swing. The 1850s were also a period of excitement in the town of Oxford as a consequence of the emergence of a number of new colleges alongside Miami.

One had already appeared, the Oxford Theological Seminary, a seminary of the Associate Reformed Church, which was closely allied with the Presbyterian Church. It was housed in a building that still stands on a street appropriately called Church Street. Anyone who walks along Church Street today will pass the building of the Oxford Theological Seminary, still commonly referred to as the Seminary, across the street from the McCullough-Hyde Hospital. High on its steeple is a date plaque that clearly reads A.D. 1838. This seminary, established for the preparation of future ministers, would be joined in 1849 by the Oxford Female Institute, the first of three women's colleges in town.

Miami, a school for men only from its day of chartering in 1809, was still restricted to male enrollment through the 1850s. The impetus for female education came from a man, John Witherspoon Scott, a close friend and associate of the first president, Robert Hamilton Bishop. Scott built a new building for the Oxford Female Institute at the corner of High and College, which survives today as a residence hall of Miami called Oxford College. Professor Scott was Miami's first science professor and accompanied Dr. Bishop to Cincinnati after Dr. Bishop's firing. Both men taught in the old Farmer's College, but in 1849, Dr. Scott came back to Oxford to establish the first female institute in the community, one of the very first indeed in the nation.

Professor Scott was affiliated with what was then referred to as the First Presbyterian Church of Oxford. By this time a Second Presbyterian Church had emerged, implying that there were theological distinctions between the First and the Second summed up as the Old School of Theology and the New School of Theology. The division between Presbyterians reflected not only theological differences, but also differences of opinion on the suitability to the Presbyterian Church of a plan of union that had been worked out at the turn of the century with the Congregational Churches of America.

Simply stated, the plan of union between the Congregationalists and the Presbyterians had called for cooperation between these two denominations rather than competition for members. The Presbyterians agreed not to compete with the Congregationalists in New England and in those areas where New Englanders were dominant, such as the Western Reserve in northeastern Ohio. In turn, the Congregationalists promised not to compete with the Presbyterians in areas of Presbyterian dominance such as Virginia and the Ohio Valley. The Presbyterian groups in America had begun by 1850 to clash over whether or not the plan of union should continue to be observed. Out of this conflict emerged a Second Presbyterian Church in Oxford, with the Rev. Daniel Tenney as its minister.

The Second Presbyterian Church decided to establish a related school for young ladies, and gave it the name of the Western Female Seminary. Though Western was on the east side of Oxford and was east of Miami University as well, it was called Western because it was west of the Mount Holyoke Female Seminary in South Hadley, Massachusetts. Western College in Oxford became the western outpost of Mount Holyoke, and by 1853, there were two women's colleges in town: one established by John Witherspoon Scott and related to the First Presbyterian Church of Oxford, the other established by the Rev. Daniel Tenney and related to the Second Presbyterian Church of Oxford. The Western Female Seminary drew to Oxford as its headmistress Miss Helen Peabody, a graduate of the Mount Holyoke Female Seminary in Massachusetts, whose first seven appointments were all graduates of Mount Holyoke. And so, as Dr. Bishop had earlier pronounced his intention that Miami should become the Yale of the West, Western College for Women became the Mount Holyoke of the West.

But there was more to come for women's education in Oxford in the 1850s. In 1856, a third women's college was established in the extreme northeasternmost corner of Oxford, called the Oxford Female College. Its first president was the former president of the Oxford Female Institute, John Witherspoon Scott, who accepted the presidency of the Oxford Female College after a dispute with the trustees of the Oxford Female Institute. By this time, a Third Presbyterian Church had emerged in town. The Oxford Female College would be supported by the Third Presbyterian Church, as Western College for Women was supported by the Second, and as the Oxford Female Institute was supported by the First. To add to the confusion, the Oxford Theological Seminary, with support from the Associate Reformed Church, emerged at mid-century as a United Presbyterian Church School. The Associate Reformed Church had merged with another Presbyterian body to become the United Presbyterian Church, and so Oxford really had four Presbyterian Churches: the United, the First, the Second, and the Third, each with its own college. It was unusual for a town of approximately 1,000 people to have five colleges, but that was what happened in Oxford in the 1850s; there were four Presbyterian churches, with a seminary and three schools for young ladies, and there was Miami University, a school for men only, but all of whose presidents had been Presbyterian ministers. It was an exciting time to be in Oxford, when so many new colleges were being created, and it could be said that Oxford at mid-century was no longer a college town: it had become a town of colleges.

In 1854, after five years of outstanding service to Miami, William C. Anderson announced his intention of returning to the Presbyterian ministry. He would leave behind a school that once more was one of the largest in the country. By the last year of his administration, 1854, Miami had 266 students, the highest enrollment Miami would achieve in the nineteenth century. With Dr. Anderson's departure, there was a search for a new president, and he was found in Huntsville, Alabama. His name was John W. Hall, and he had served as minister of a Presbyterian congregation in Huntsville. John W. Hall is remembered today on the Miami campus by Hall Auditorium. He was a Southerner, born in North Carolina, raised in Tennessee, and serving an Alabama church when called to Oxford. He would be Miami's president from 1854 until 1866, a twelve-year period, in the middle of which the Civil War erupted, pitting the North against the South. President Hall was suspected of Confederate sympathy because of his Southern background, but his loyalty to the Union never wavered. Indeed, Miami was fortunate to have as its leader during the War Between the States a man of the stature and the wisdom of John W. Hall.

Though there were many causes of the Civil War, eventually there was Secession, and Miami University was torn apart by it. Miami had students from the South as well as from the North when on Saturday morning, April 13, 1861, news was received that in the harbor of Charleston, South Carolina, Confederate shore batteries had bombarded Fort Sumter. The students and faculty of Miami gathered together in chapel on the second floor of the Old Main academic building, where Harrison Hall stands today, there to hear the words of President Hall announcing that he had received the news of the bombardment of Fort Sumter. The Civil War had begun, dividing the nation as it divided Miami University.

Miami was situated only thirty-seven miles from the Ohio River, a river designated by the Northwest Ordinance of 1787 as the historic boundary line between free soil north of the river and slave soil to the south. Miami University was therefore only thirty-seven miles from slavery, and its student body, its faculty, and even its president represented the South as well as the North. There had been conflicting opinions on campus over the rightness or wrongness of slavery, and among Miami presidents, clearly the first, Dr. Bishop, the third, Erasmus McMaster, and the fourth, William Anderson, all had Northern points of view and abolitionist sympathies. On the other hand, George Junkin, our second president, had in the brief time of his presidency, from 1841 to 1844, spoken publicly in Hamilton in favor of slavery, and after he left Miami in 1844, he became president of what was then called Washington University in Lexington, Virginia, which was eventually renamed, after the Civil War, Washington and Lee. His oldest daughter, Eleanor, had married Stonewall Jackson, at that time a Mathematics instructor at the Virginia Military Institute, making Junkin the father-in-law of Robert E. Lee's most trusted general in the Confederate Army.

It was a further complication that the President of

Miami when the Civil War began was John Hall, a Southerner from North Carolina, Tennessee, and Alabama. Hall was in favor of states' rights, but his loyalty to the Union was unswerving, despite the suspicion his Southern background aroused. So there were sectional differences among the Miami presidents, and there were comparable differences among the faculty and students. One of the early Miami instructors was Albert Taylor Bledsoe, a graduate of the United States Military Academy at West Point, and a Virginian, who, when the war came, served the South as Assistant Secretary of War in the Cabinet of Jefferson Davis. In 1863, Albert Bledsoe became Special Commissioner to Great Britain for the Confederate States of America, and made a vain effort to persuade England to declare itself on the side of the South in the fight against the North.

Albert Taylor Bledsoe reflected a pro-Southern sentiment in the Miami faculty, but there was an equally outspoken faculty member on the opposite side, Robert White McFarland, also a mathematician. Professor McFarland later became President of Miami, but in 1862, he organized a regiment of Miami students, the 86th Ohio, to support the preservation of the Union.

Increasing the division between presidents and faculty members over the Civil War was a similar division within the student body. When the war broke out in April of 1861, Miami had among its students the representatives of five Southern states. Miami had become a national university even then, with a student body drawn from both North and South, and in fact twenty-five percent of the student body came from south of the Ohio River at the time of the Civil War, a larger Southern proportion than at any time since. The regional diversity of Miami was reflected in the division of opinion among presidents, faculty, and students, and when war was announced on Saturday morning, April 13, 1861, in the chapel meeting at Old

Main, President Hall advised Miami students to do nothing precipitous, to go back to their rooms, and to think through what they should do individually in response to the war that was now upon them all. He then adjourned the chapel meeting.

The chapel was cleared, and shortly after noon, it filled again, this time with students and a number of townsmen, primarily young men, called into special meeting by a senior in the Miami student body by the name of Ozro J. Dodds. Ozro Dodds, from Cincinnati, had come to Miami as a transfer student from Wabash College in Crawsfordsville, Indiana. He addressed about 160 students gathered there in chapel, and said he didn't know what they proposed to do, but he knew what he proposed to do. He proposed to give his services to the Governor of the State of Ohio, William Dennison, Miami class of 1835, as a volunteer to serve in putting down the rebellion in the South. He passed a sheet of paper around the room, saying those who wished could sign their names to join him in the formation of a military company, which he proposed to name the University Rifles, which would begin drilling in preparation for military service the following Monday morning. The sheet was passed around the room; all 160 signed their names. That was the first day of the Civil War, Saturday, April 13, 1861. The Sunday following was quiet across the campus, and then on Monday morning, the drilling began. Under the leadership of Ozro Dodds, the 160 Miami students and townsmen banded together as the University Rifle Company, and they began to drill together, using tree branches and broomsticks instead of guns, on the north side of the main academic building.

On the south side of the same building, students and young townsmen sympathetic to the cause of the Confederacy also began to drill. While the men of Miami and the young men of the town drilled on opposite sides of Old Main, the young women of the three women's colleges gathered in the home of Orange Nash Stoddard on Campus Avenue, the home today occupied by the United Campus Ministry. They began to sew a giant American flag, using materials Professor Stoddard had brought up from Cincinnati, putting together an enormous flag that would display thirty-three states. There were thirty-three states in the former Union, and thirty-three in the Union they hoped to save. Twenty-two states joined the North in the Civil War, and eleven states joined the South. As the young women sewed this huge American flag, they also began to sew shirts of red cloth to be worn by Miami men going into combat.

The drilling on campus by young men and the sewing of the flag and the shirts by young women continued through the following week, until Friday, the 19th of April, when Abraham Lincoln, the President of the United States, finally issued his call for volunteers to put down the rebellion in the South. While Lincoln called for 75,000 volunteers for ninety days of service, Jefferson Davis, the President of the Confederate States of America, issued a similar appeal to the supporters of the South. Each side, both North and South, believed the war would be a short one, only ninety days at most until the fighting would end. The young men of Miami prepared to leave the campus—at any rate the juniors and seniors, leaving behind only sophomores, freshmen, and the boys in the preparatory department. On Monday, April 22, the men of Miami marched side by side to the little railroad station on Elm Street, where they boarded the train that would take them to Hamilton, twelve miles to the east. When they descended to the platform at Hamilton, they said good-bye to their roommates, fraternity brothers, and best friends, and parted ways.

The Miami men sympathetic to the North took the next train from Hamilton north to Columbus, where they would proceed to Camp Jackson, to be sworn in as Company B of the 20th Ohio Volunteer Infantry Regiment. The Miami men sympathetic to the South would take the next train headed south for Cincinnati. There they would transfer to yet another train that would take them across the Ohio, through Kentucky, and down to Nashville, where they would go their separate ways into regiments of the Confederacy. Many of these good friends and former roommates would meet again, almost a year to the day later, at a place called Shiloh on the Tennessee River, where they would fight on opposite sides in the Battle of Shiloh, sometimes called the Battle of Pittsburg Landing. There, the armies of the South under Generals Johnston and Beauregard faced the armies of the North under General Ulysses S. Grant.

The fighting began on Easter Sunday, April 6, 1862. It continued for the next two days, and in the course of the fighting, the 81st Ohio regiment swept over a Tennessee regiment identified as the 20th. The 81st Ohio was made up mainly of those who had been originally in the 20th Ohio, including Company B, the University Rifle Company from Miami, which had signed up as volunteers for ninety days. The war was obviously lasting much longer, and the 81st had signed up again for three years of service, knowing the war would go on at least that long. When the 81st Ohio regiment defeated the 20th Tennessee regiment on the bloody battlefield of Shiloh, they captured the colonel in command, whose name was appropriately Battle. As the colonel was being taken behind the lines, he heard his captors talking about Miami in Oxford. He called out to ask them, "Are you the Oxford Company?" and they said they were. He then asked, "Do you know my son, Joel, a member of Beta Theta Pi at Miami?" They said they did, and so Colonel Battle pled with them, "My son has fallen out there in the field. Will you find him and bury him?" The men of the

Oxford Company searched the battle ground until they found the body of Joel Battle. Two of his Beta Theta Pi fraternity brothers, Cliff Ross and J.C. Lewis, buried him where he had fallen, and his remains lie there to this day. The war pitted brother against brother, friend against friend, and Miami men against Miami men, but they still could be loyal to each other.

Miami was indeed involved in the Civil War, perhaps more than any other American college, since it had so many students and faculty on both sides of the conflict. Of the ten members of Lincoln's Cabinet, two were from Miami: Secretary of the Interior Caleb Blood Smith and Postmaster General William Dennison. When the Civil War began, there were five governors of thirty-three states who were Miami graduates: the Governor of Ohio, the Governor of Indiana, the Governor of Illinois, the Governor of Michigan, and the Governor of Mississippi. In addition, Ohio would have two Civil War governors from this small campus, Missouri would have two governors just after the war, Iowa would have one Miami governor, and California one Miami governor just before the war. Then there were the generals who led the armies, north and south. Ten Union generals were graduates of Miami, including Benjamin Harrison, class of 1852, who would later become the 23rd President of the United States. Three Confederate generals were Miami graduates, including Joseph Davis, class of 1842, from Mississippi, nephew of President Jefferson Davis of the Confederate States of America. And there were even admirals, because the Civil War was the first war in which submarines and iron-clad naval vessels were used. There were only three admirals in the Union Navy, and two of them were Miamians; the highest ranking was Stephen C. Rowan, for whom Rowan Hall, across from the Sesquicentennial Chapel, is named today. This was the same Stephen Rowan who had led the marines ashore in

California in the war with Mexico, and he was the first to put the flag of the United States in the soil of California and claim it for this nation.

There were also Civil War spies from Oxford, most notably Charlotte, nicknamed "Lottie," Moon, who eventually married Jim Clark, a Miami graduate. Her family lived in a home that is still called the Lottie Moon House on High Street, across from the campus. Lottie Moon was born in Virginia, and was brought to Oxford as a young girl with her two sisters and two brothers in the family of Dr. Robert Moon, a physician. Lottie Moon was, in 1849, briefly engaged to be married to Ambrose E. Burnside, an officer in the United States Army. But Burnside, who was from Liberty, Indiana, was jilted by Lottie at the altar of a little church in Brownsville, Indiana, not many miles from Oxford. She deserted him because she really wanted to marry Jim Clark, a fellow Virginian, and eventually Lottie and Jim would be married. When the war broke out, Lottie's two brothers, Bob and Bill, would join the Confederate Army and Navy. Lottie herself served as an espionage agent for the South, being a gifted actress who could easily don a garb and feign an accent, pretending to be a titled English noblewoman on one occasion or an Irish washerwoman on another.

On her first memorable occasion, in the fall of 1862, after meeting with a group of Southern sympathizers in Toronto, Canada, Lottie Moon was sent south to report the results of that meeting, which had been plotting how to find a way of splitting the Midwest off from the rest of the northern states. She boldly presented herself at the office of Edwin M. Stanton, an Ohioan who was Lincoln's Secretary of War, announcing herself as Lady Hull, an English noblewoman, who was suffering from acute rheumatic arthritis. In her best English accent, Lottie Moon told Secretary Stanton how she had traveled across the ocean not knowing there was a war on, and was prevented by the inconvenience of the war from going further to seek relief at the warm springs of Virginia. She implored the Secretary of War to help her, and Secretary Stanton was so moved by her impassioned plea that he suggested to Lady Hull that the next day, when President Abraham Lincoln himself was going to visit his troops in the field, she ride with him to the front lines, where she could cross the lines with a pass that he, Edwin Stanton, would give her, and then she could bathe in the warm springs of Virginia and relieve her arthritic distress. Lottie Moon accepted the invitation, and next day found herself seated in a carriage next to the President of the United States, across from the Secretary of War. As the carriage rumbled through the northern Virginia hills, Lady Hull pretended to fall asleep, and as she dozed, President Lincoln and Secretary Stanton talked openly about their plans for carrying on the war. She slept until they got to the front lines, and then awoke to take the pass that Secretary Stanton had given her and cross the lines into Richmond for a rendezvous with President Jefferson Davis himself.

It became obvious during the next several weeks that the war was going disastrously for the North, as though the South knew every enemy move that was about to take place. Then the President and the Secretary of War realized they had been duped, and that Lady Hull was not an English noblewoman, but Lottie Moon, a Confederate spy, in whose apparently sleeping presence they had discussed their secret strategy for conducting the war. Secretary Stanton put a price of $10,000 on Lottie's head, dead or alive. She would be caught the following April, 1863, in Cincinnati, disguised as an Irish washerwoman seeking safe passage across the Ohio River to get to Lexington, Kentucky, in order to see—so she said—her injured son lying in a hospital. But she met a new private just assigned to his post, who refused to let her pass. Lottie Moon asked in her best Irish brogue if she could be permitted to cross the Ohio River into Kentucky, but the private told her only the general could give such permission. "Then take me to the General," said Lottie.

The private proceeded to take her up a flight of stairs to an office on the second floor, where after knocking on the door, he escorted her inside. Seated behind the desk was the new officer in Command of the Defense of Southern Ohio and Southeastern Indiana, in his splendid uniform of Union blue with gold stars: none other than General Ambrose E. Burnside. The Irish brogue stuck in Lottie's throat, but she attempted to explain to the General why she needed safe passage across the Ohio River into Kentucky. After a few minutes of listening to her change her accent from Irish to English to Southern and back again, Ambrose Burnside said, "You can stop it, Lottie. I know who you are." Lottie denied she'd ever met him before, but General Burnside said she most certainly had met him, and in fact, she had almost become his wife. At that point, Lottie broke down and began to cry. General Burnside could easily have turned Lottie over for arrest and probable hanging as a spy, but he still had a spark of love for her, despite his having been jilted by her years earlier at the altar in Indiana. He ordered her sent to the Burnet House in Cincinnati for house arrest, on her solemn promise that she would never spy again; this time she kept her promise, and thus the war was over for Lottie Moon in April 1863.

The war ended for everyone else two years afterward, in April, 1865, at Appomattox Court House in Virginia. The Army of Northern Virginia, under Robert E. Lee, surrendered to the armies of the United States under the command of General Ulysses S. Grant, and a little later the men of Miami who had survived the war would slowly begin to return to the campus to resume their studies. The war was finally over, but for Miami, the hardship was just beginning. Before many years had elapsed, Miami would have to close its doors and extinguish its lights. There had been 516 American colleges when the war started; only 104 were able to keep going after it was over. Miami was one that did not survive.

CHAPTER VIII

OLD MIAMI DIES, NEW MIAMI IS BORN

It was on the 10th of April, 1865, that news reached Oxford and Miami University of the surrender of the Army of Northern Virginia, commanded by General Robert E. Lee, to the Union forces under the leadership of Ulysses S. Grant, at a place called Appomattox Court House in Virginia. The Civil War was effectively over, ending the most costly and bloody conflict in American history, with casualties exceeding all the other losses in all the other wars fought by the United States, from colonial times to the War of 1812, the War with Mexico, the War with Spain, World War I, World War II, the Vietnam Conflict, the Korean Conflict, and the Gulf War. All the casualties of all those wars do not equal the losses sustained by this nation in the Civil War of 1861-1865.

As Walter Havinghurst has written, "On April 10, 1865, came the news from Appomattox, and Oxford's church bells rang through the twilight, candles glimmered on High Street, a bonfire blazed beside the market house. Next morning, at the sound of the chapel bell, students and townspeople streamed over the campus paths. President John W. Hall spoke briefly and gravely of the nation's sufferings and then closed with a troubled prayer of thanksgiving, and a prayer that the land would never again be darkened and the college divided by fratricidal war. As the *Miami Monthly* put it, 'While many students at other colleges have given up their books and gone off in some military company, yet we know of no college either east or west which has sent out in a body such a number to represent us in this war.' Now some of the Miami boys would return with men's lines in their faces, taking up their Greek and Logic while Shiloh and Chickamauga slowly sank into memory."

There are still reminders on the Miami campus of those who participated in the Civil War. Dodds Hall was named for Ozro Dodds, the senior and editor of the student newspaper who organized the University Rifles to fight as part of the 20th Ohio volunteer infantry regiment. McFarland Hall bears the name of Robert White McFarland, mathematics professor, who, a year after the University Rifles went off to war, led the younger boys of Oxford and Miami into combat as the 86th Ohio Regiment in the fall of 1862. And Harrison Hall is a reminder of Benjamin Harrison, one of the ten Union generals who graduated from this university, a member of the class of 1852 who later became the 23rd President of the United States. Then there is Rowan Hall, across from the Sesquicentennial Chapel, which commemorates Admiral Stephen Rowan, class of 1828, who led the Marines ashore in California at the beginning of the War with Mexico and claimed California for the United States, and who in the 1860s was the highest ranking Admiral of the United States Navy. There is also Dennison Hall, named for William Dennison, class of 1835, Governor of Ohio when the war began and later Postmaster General in Abraham Lincoln's Cabinet. When we pass Hall Auditorium, we remember John W. Hall, Miami President at the time of the Civil War. Nor should we forget Lottie Moon, the Confederate spy who once lived in the house now called the Lottie Moon House, across the street from the campus at the corner of University and High. She could be called one of the few female participants in the war. All of these names evoke memories of the War Between the States, a war fought between brothers, some of them classmates from the same college.

When the Civil War ended, only 104 colleges out of 516 American colleges would survive, and Miami was one of the 412 that were unable to continue. And so we call the period from its Charter in 1809 through the Civil War to its closing in 1873 the period of the Old Miami. The college was closed for twelve years, from 1873 to 1885, and since 1885 it has been the New Miami.

There are a number of ways to explain why Miami was forced to close in 1873, but the most obvious explanation is the impact of the Civil War. Miami was an all-male college, like most of the other American colleges at that time, and it sent most of its students into military service, in either the 20th Ohio regiment in 1861, or the 86th Ohio in 1862, or in the Confederate army. There were not enough students left to generate the necessary income through student fees to keep the bills paid, and after the war ended, Miami was not able to enroll more than a total of 166 students, though in the 1850s its enrollment had reached over 250. The aftermath of war brought the enrollment down to a final 87 students in 1872-73, forcing Miami to close its doors.

Part of the reason for closing was a direct result of the war, since Miami had always had a solid group of students from the South, usually averaging about twenty-five percent, or one-fourth, of the total enrollment. There was no Southern contingent left after the war, nor has there been a substantial one since. Old Miami, after the Civil War, enrolled less than one percent of its students from the South. Miami University simply could not recover from the Civil War, and by 1873, it was bankrupt.

Another cause of closing, however, was the old-fashioned curriculum. Miami, like many of the colleges that did not survive the war, had retained its traditional classical curriculum, with heavy emphasis on Latin, Greek, and Hebrew. The nation around it was changing rapidly, and the industrialization which enabled the North to defeat the South was accelerating, increasing the need for practical arts and for a more scientific curriculum. The Classical Humanities curriculum was one of the victims of the Civil

War, and Miami suffered from holding on to it too long.

Nor should it be forgotten that Miami remained a male college after the war and resisted co-education. Most of the 412 colleges that closed after the war were all-male, but the new female colleges never stopped. All three women's colleges in Oxford kept right on going during the war and after. There were a few co-educational colleges which had started before the war, and these also continued without interruption, notably Oberlin College in Ohio. If Miami had admitted women earlier, it might have survived, but it refused to change and remained a campus for men only until it was forced to close in 1873.

Miami was also troubled by a succession of fairly weak leaders in the period surrounding the Civil War. John W. Hall had been president during and immediately after the war, succeeded by Robert Livingston Stanton, and finally by Andrew Dousa Hepburn, Stanton's successor. None of these presidents had been able to give Miami strong leadership when it was needed.

The problem with John Hall was that he was a Southerner, and the South lost the Civil War. Though he was outspokenly loyal to the Union, to many he was always suspect simply because he was known to be of Southern background. By 1866, he himself concluded that his time of usefulness at Miami had come to an end and he voluntarily submitted his resignation in the spring of 1866.

He was replaced by Robert Livingston Stanton, who served as Miami president from 1866 to 1871, nominated for the position by the chairman of the Board of Trustees, John W. Herron of Cincinnati. Herron's daughter, Nellie, married William Howard Taft, later a President of the United States. So the father-in-law of the man who was to become President Taft suggested as the successor to John Hall a theological professor in a Presbyterian seminary in Danville, Kentucky, Robert Livingston Stanton, and the

Board went along with the chairman's suggestion.

Robert Livingston Stanton seemed a good choice. He brought a certain national visibility to Miami, since his brother, Henry Brewster Stanton, was one of the leading abolitionist leaders in the Civil War. His sister-in-law was even more prominent, for the wife of Henry Brewster Stanton was Elizabeth Cady Stanton, an early leader in the crusade to achieve equal rights for women, which had begun with Women's Suffrage in the nineteenth century. The name of Elizabeth Cady Stanton was second only to Susan B. Anthony as an early leader of women's causes.

Just imagine the excitement at Miami and in Oxford when the sister-in-law of the president of the university arrived to give a talk to the faculty and students. So President Stanton started with a family advantage, in the fact that he was the brother of a well-known Abolitionist and brother-in-law of a nationally prominent Suffragette who occasionally visited the campus. During his administration, some construction was undertaken on campus, including the replacement of the west wing of the Old Main academic building. The cornerstone of the building had been laid in 1816, but fifty years later it was badly in need of repair, and it was torn down in 1867 and a new structure put in its place by 1870. The new wing would last until 1958 when the entire building was demolished.

President Stanton also built a home at the corner of Oak and Spring which survives today as the Bonham House, but for years it was called the Stanton House. There had been no presidential home since the old log school that had been improved for President Bishop and his family. All the presidents after him had lived in town, but President Stanton thought the time had come for the Miami President to live in the heart of the campus and he selected the site for his home with that in mind. It was paid for by President Stanton out of his own funds, but since he lived in it for such a brief time, he did not have time to finish the payment of his loan, and after he left town, the house was acquired by others until finally it ended in the possession of the first President of the New Miami, Robert White McFarland. Bonham House continued to be the home of the Miami president when President McFarland later succeeded President Stanton, but his daughter, Frances, "Fanny," inherited it, and she married Llewellyn Bonham. For the rest of the nineteenth and well into the twentieth century, the Bonham family lived in the house, and ultimately it came to be called Bonham House. The Bonham name is familiar in Oxford, since there is also a Bonham Road that leads out of town from the northeast corner of the old square mile.

The Stanton years were not all bad; they deserve to be credited with replacement of the west wing of Old Main, and the construction of a presidential home, Bonham House, presently occupied by the Campus Security office. Two student publications also emerged at this time. One was *The Miami Student* and the other was the *Recensio.* When you pick up a copy of *The Miami Student* today, you read under the masthead that it is the oldest college newspaper in the United States, established in 1826. True, if you count the years that there was a student publication before 1867, *The Miami Student* is the oldest college newspaper in the land. But to make the masthead statement literally true, you have to regard *The Monthly Literary Focus* which began in 1827 as the original of *The Miami Student,* although it was a literary publication rather than an account of student happenings on campus. *The Miami Student* as a publication with that name actually started in 1867, forty years later. The first Miami yearbook, called *The Recensio,* was published initially in 1869. Its name is Latin, meaning "Looking Back." *The Miami Student* in 1867 and *The Recensio* in 1869 were publications that began while Stanton was president and that are still being published today.

Thus there are positives to be reckoned with in the administration of President Stanton; there were negatives as well, and these ultimately would cause him to resign in frustration in 1871. In the year 1866, when he became president, Miami had an enrollment of 166, but a steady decline brought it down to around 100 by the time he resigned in 1871. Not that he wasn't trying to revive the university after the Civil War had brought it to the brink of bankruptcy, but the directions he sought to take were unavailing.

He first tried to convert it from a state institution to a private religious college under the auspices of the Presbyterian Church, pointing out that every president of Miami had been a Presbyterian clergyman. Not only the president but the faculty were Presbyterian ministers, and for many years, Miami had been the principal source of Presbyterian clergymen for the State of Ohio. Moreover, the town of Oxford had four Presbyterian churches with four colleges linked to them. President Stanton, who was himself a Presbyterian minister, felt that Miami should seek further church support. In 1866, the synod of the Presbyterian Church of Ohio announced its intention to give financial support to a college, and President Stanton petitioned the synod to accept Miami as a Presbyterian school. The synod met, deliberated, and in its wisdom decided not to accept the petition of Miami, but rather to start an entirely new college in the town of Wooster which would be formally named the College of Wooster and would be supported by the Presbyterian Church.

Stymied in his first attempt to save Miami, President Stanton tried another tack. He knew that an act of Congress had come during the Civil War years, authored by Senator Justin Morrill of Vermont. The Morrill Act of 1862 had proposed to give federal support to each State of the Union in direct relation to the number of congressmen and senators from each state, contingent on the introduction of college programs in agricultural and mechanical sciences. The Morrill Act was a deliberate attempt to foster the practical arts and sciences instead of the old Classical Humanities curriculum.

Ohio had at that time nineteen United States representatives and two senators for a total of twenty-one members of Congress. The Morrill Act proposed to grant 30,000 acres of federal land for every Congressman, and so Ohio was entitled to 630,000 acres of federal land to be sold or leased, with the income to support an Agricultural and Mechanical program. The earlier Act of Congress in 1792, which led to Miami's charter, set aside a single college township of six miles square or 23,000 acres in the Symmes Purchase. The Morrill Act promised 630,000 acres for an Ohio college, many times more than the original Miami grant, and so President Stanton applied for Miami to become the agricultural and mechanical college of Ohio. President Stanton was perfectly serious in his application, because Miami was, and is, located in the heart of an agricultural region, but he was not the only applicant. The state legislature had to determine which one of several applicants would be funded under the Morrill Act, and understandably, it decided in favor of establishing a wholly new school near the state capitol building in Columbus.

The Ohio Agricultural and Mechanical College was chartered in 1870 in Columbus, and for eight years, it continued under that name. But since it drew very few agricultural students, there was great pressure for it to become a multi-faceted, multi-dimensional college offering a wide curriculum. The trustees voted in 1878 to change the name to The Ohio State University and add the liberal arts to its curriculum, along with agriculture and engineering. Today, Ohio State owns acres of grain and orchards, and pastures for horses, cattle, sheep, swine, and chickens, as part of a campus surrounded by the city of Columbus. But the College of Agriculture at Ohio State has shifted much of its emphasis on research to the Wooster Agricultural Experiment Station in Wooster, Ohio, and most agriculture students are educated there. President Stanton hoped Miami would become the Ohio Agricultural and Mechanical College, but he failed to realize his hope.

But President Stanton was not discouraged in his efforts to keep Miami going as a viable institution after the Civil War. He noted that Miami had produced ten Union generals and three Confederate generals among its graduates, and that most of the student body had gone to fight in the war. He became convinced that Miami was the right place to develop military leadership, and argued for converting the college into a military school, on the order of the Citadel in South Carolina or the Virginia Military Institute in Virginia. President Stanton envisioned Miami as the Citadel or VMI of Ohio, changing it into an Ohio Military College.

So, for the academic year 1869-70, he appointed a Civil War officer by the name of Caleb Carlton to the faculty, with the aim of establishing a military science program. Students were recruited to enroll in it, and Colonel Carlton came to the Miami campus with a Civil War cannon in tow, symbolic of the new emphasis on the military at Miami. But unfortunately, accusations followed Colonel Carlton to Miami, and he had to answer charges that he had misused commissary funds in Wyoming Territory during the Civil War. He was obliged to go to Omaha to face the charges, and the military science program at Miami foundered in his absence. Once again, President Stanton had failed to rescue Miami from bankruptcy.

Something however became of the cannon which Colonel Carlton brought to the campus. One April evening in 1870, a group of students undertook to wheel the cannon off the Miami campus, across what is now called Patterson Avenue, and up the hill on the campus of Miss Peabody's Western Female Seminary. They brought it into position squarely facing the front doors of what is today Peabody Hall. They loaded it with a full charge of powder, and at midnight, they touched a match to it: the Miami cannon roared. Instantly, lights appeared in the hall, and the women of Western came to their windows to see what had caused the explosion. With the light of their candles and kerosene lamps they peered out of the windows, when who should appear at the front door but Miss Peabody herself in a night shirt and night cap. She was furious, and shouted to the young men of Miami to get off the Western property at once, or she would see that every one of them was expelled. They could see that she meant it, and so off they went, leaving the cannon behind. Next morning, when the women of Western awoke, the cannon was still in position before the doors of Miss Peabody's hall. They knew what to do: the women of Western simply turned the cannon 180 degrees and gave it a push, and gravity did the rest. The men of Miami had pushed the cannon up the hill slowly the night before, but the following morning it went down the hill on its own at accelerating speed. At the bottom of the hill, it splashed into the duck pond and sank from sight. When the cannon disappeared into the duck pond, it symbolized the end of the military program at Miami, and another failure for President Stanton.

But he did not give up. He next turned to the legislature of the State of Ohio and asked for funding to establish a law college at Miami. The legislature again deliberated and refused the Miami offer, saying that legal education ought to take place in a larger community than Oxford. So President Stanton had failed four times to make Miami a different kind of college to survive, and though he was full of ideas and energy, he virtually wore himself out in five years on campus, since he was a teacher as well as a college president. One student, at the time of his commencement in 1871, recalled that in his four years at Miami, he had President Stanton in fifteen different courses, and he had heard President Stanton give at least seventy major addresses in chapel. The end had to come for him, and in the spring of 1871, President Stanton tendered his resignation and departed to take a newspaper job with the *New York Independent* in New York City.

But the trustees had not given up, and in a final effort to save the college, they selected a faculty member, Professor Andrew Dousa Hepburn, to be the new President. Andrew Hepburn lasted just two years, from 1871 to 1873. He had come to Miami as the first Professor of English Language and Literature in 1868, and he was promoted to President in 1871. But President Hepburn turned out to be the last President of Old Miami, the seventh consecutive Presbyterian minister at the head of the institution. He was an outspoken foe of co-education, and defender of the old classical curriculum which had characterized Miami education from its beginning. In his second year, 1872-73, enrollment sagged to 87, a figure so low that the trustees, in the spring of 1873, determined that Miami would hold its last commencement and then would close. It did so in 1873, and in most of the twelve years that followed, the buildings were either empty or were used, as in the period from 1877 to 1885, to house a private preparatory school run by two men, Byron Marsh and Isaiah Trufant, which was called the Miami Classical and Scientific Training School. It was a modest educational mission but was better than nothing, helping the Old Miami mark time, until at long last the New Miami could re-open as a university in 1885.

Chapter IX

A TOWN OF COLLEGES
BECOMES A COLLEGE TOWN

The New Miami began on September 17, 1885, when, as Walter Havighurst has noted, "every carriage, trap and buggy in Oxford went to the railroad depot to meet the morning train." There were hundreds of visitors in town for the re-opening of Miami University; flags lined High Street; there were flowers in front of the shops, and Chinese lanterns swung in the autumn breeze. A sign of welcome hung on the corner of the campus where the slant walk led from town, because twelve years after they had closed, the doors of Miami University were once again open.

Other festivities were held: a picnic supper on the grounds, newly mown for the opening, and the ringing of the college bell from the roof of Old Main amid the clanging of church bells from across the town. The noise of tin pans being banged and of fire-crackers exploding accompanied a procession of people—visitors, villagers, alumni and new students—all marching across the campus and up High Street. A bonfire was lit in the public square, where the crowd heard speeches from the trustees and the new president, Robert White McFarland.

The college debts had been paid, and an additional $50,000 had been raised as a permanent endowment for the revived university. Calvin Brice of the class of 1863, who had made a fortune building railroads, underwrote two professorships, and the State of Ohio had appropriated $26,000 for current expenses and the repair of the university buildings. Except for tuition paid for Civil War veterans in what could be called the first G.I. Bill, this money was the first appropriation from the Ohio legislature for Miami University. It would grow from a mere $26,000 in 1885 to more than $63 million in 1995-96.

The principal speech given on the eve of Miami's re-opening was delivered by Robert Hamilton Bishop, Jr., "Old Bobby," one of the living links between Old Miami and New, the son of the first Miami President. He had, in the year before the re-opening of the college, taught a class of twelve prospective freshmen so that they would be ready to enroll at the New Miami to get the new college underway. He held his class in a room of what we now call Elliott Hall, while the other rooms were being rented for the classical and scientific training school of Messrs. Trufant and Marsh. Other speakers that September evening in 1885 were the new President, Robert White McFarland, and the former President, Andrew Dousa Hepburn. All three of these men, Bishop, McFarland, and Hepburn, had taught together at the Old Miami until its closure in 1873, and now twelve years later, they were back on campus to preside over the launching of the New Miami.

The New Miami had a total enrollment in the fall of 1885 of forty, twenty of whom were in the preparatory department, twenty at the collegiate level. The university was the recipient of state funds totaling $26,000, which included $20,000 for the repair of buildings and $6,000 for operating expenses. The new President, Dr. McFarland, had been a mathematics professor in the Old Miami, but he had come back to the New Miami as the first layman president in the history of the school, since all seven of his predecessors had been Presbyterian ministers. Dr. McFarland had been a militant Unionist in the time of the Civil War, and had led a regiment into combat as its colonel. He had raised the 86th Ohio Volunteer Infantry Regiment almost entirely from Miami students and led it into battle in 1862. After the Civil War, he had returned to Miami to continue to instruct mathematics until its closure in 1873, and then

17. President Guy Potter Benton, 1902-11, who was the only Methodist minister to serve as Miami President, following a succession of Presbyterian ministers

18. The first Hepburn Hall, a women's dormitory built in 1905 and named for a notorious foe of co-education at Miami, torn down later to make way for King Library and for a second Hepburn Hall, a men's dormitory (Postcard by the Oxford Printing Co.)

19. President Raymond Mollyneaux Hughes, 1911-27, a farmer's son who became Professor of Chemistry and then President of Miami

20. The Poet's Shack in the woods east of the main campus, built for Percy MacKaye, the first Poet-in-Residence on an American university campus

21. Wallace Roudebush, Business Manager and Treasurer of Miami, for whom Roudebush Hall is named, and George Rider, Coach and Director of Athletics, Father of "The Cradle of Coaches"

22. President Alfred Horatio Upham, 1928-45, Professor of English, who wrote the Centennial history, ***Old Miami, the Yale of the Early West,*** *and the Alma Mater, "Old Miami," and who served longest as Miami president (16 1/2 years)*

23. Co-eds exercising in Herron Gymnasium, built with a running track around the inner walls

24. Herron Gymnasium being moved east to accommodate Ogden Hall, a women's dormitory, constructed upon the bequest of a quarter of a million dollars, with the provision that it be located west of Herron Hall (Photograph by Frank Snyder)

25. Sailors marching under the Beta Bell Tower during World War II, when Miami housed a Navy school for code operators and another for officers' training

26. After World War II, when the G.I. Bill brought many veterans to campus, temporary buildings were erected for them, nicknamed "Vet Village" and also "Fertile Valley" (Photograph by Gilson Wright, courtesy of Smith Library of Regional History, Oxford, Ohio)

27. Joseph Bachelor, Professor of English, who amassed 400 acres of farmland east of Oxford, and at his death in 1947 willed it to Miami as the Bachelor Wildlife Preserve

28. Walter Havighurst, Professor of English, author of 36 books of fiction and regional history, including ***The Miami Years,*** *the sesquicentennial history of the university (Portrait Photograph by George Hoxie)*

29. President John D. Millett, hired in 1952 as an expert in financing American higher education, who left in 1963 to become the first Chancellor of the Ohio Board of Regents (Portrait Photograph by George Hoxie)

30. Alumnus Gus Kumler, hugging a group of cheerleaders on his return to Miami at age 102

31. President Phillip R. Shriver, President 1965-81, who retired to become Professor of History; this book is based on his popular course in the History of Miami University (Portrait Photograph by George Hoxie)

32. President Paul G. Pearson, who came from Rutgers University to head Miami during the years from 1981-1992 when it was recognized as a "Public Ivy"

went to the new Ohio Agricultural and Mechanical College in Columbus. In his period of service at Ohio State, as it came to be called, he had become convinced that the future of Miami and most American colleges of the country lay in offering applied arts or practical arts along with agricultural and mechanical sciences. So when he returned to Miami from Ohio State, he sought to do away with traditional reliance on the classical curriculum of the past and install practical and applied courses of study.

Andrew Dousa Hepburn, who had been appointed as the first Professor of English Language and Literature at Miami beginning in 1868, had been the last president of Old Miami, from 1871 to 1873. When Miami closed in 1873, he had gone south to accept the presidency of Davidson College in North Carolina, but when Miami reopened in 1885, he returned to Oxford.

So the three veterans of the Old Miami, Bishop, McFarland, and Hepburn, became the mainstays of the New Miami. But though they came back as former colleagues and friends, they had divergent views of the direction the university should take. "Old Bobby" Bishop served the New Miami only two years until his retirement in 1887. But McFarland and Hepburn, both somewhat younger men, found themselves on opposite sides of the fence on most questions about the future of the school. The McFarland-Hepburn Feud, as it came to be called, began in 1885 and persisted until both men left the faculty in 1888. McFarland was strongly in favor of practical and applied courses, even supporting the prospect of an engineering department. He felt that the sciences and mathematics should dominate the New Miami curriculum, and that religion should no longer be central to higher education. He believed the time had come to abolish mandatory chapel and to cease requiring every student to participate in a worship service every day.

McFarland was also convinced that the time had come

for Miami to become co-educational. He suggested to the board of trustees that they should see if co-education might not be tried, and as the first female student to break the male barrier, he recommended his own daughter, Frances. McFarland also recommended increased enrollment of the sons and daughters of farmers in the surrounding agricultural region, and on all these points, he met with opposition from his old colleague, Andrew Dousa Hepburn.

Hepburn had served as the last president of the Old Miami, and was a professional humanist. He believed fully that the humanities ought to be central to Miami in the future as they had been in the past, and as a Professor of English Literature, he thought that the classical curriculum still mattered, that it was important to keep a primary emphasis on instruction in Latin, Greek, and Hebrew, not to change in favor of science and mathematics as McFarland was suggesting. Hepburn was also a bitter foe of co-education, seeing no reason why Miami should turn its back on the tradition of admitting males only. As a Presbyterian minister, he thought daily chapel was important for every student and every member of the faculty, and so he fought the new president's attempts to change the Miami traditions.

There was one respect in which Hepburn agreed with McFarland, and that was the encouragement of local farmers to send their children to Miami. Otherwise, they were on opposite sides of every issue, stemming in part from their involvement in the Civil War. McFarland was pro-Union and taught at Ohio State after Miami, whereas Hepburn had gone south after the war to take a position at Davidson College in North Carolina. The division between them was public and it divided the other faculty and students, forcing Bishop to retire in 1887, and then, in 1888, the board of trustees called for both McFarland and Hepburn to resign, and for the rest of the faculty to follow them. The trustees believed that only by such a clean sweep could they end the bitter division in the university and allow Miami to start afresh.

Interestingly, McFarland was never re-employed by Miami University after his dismissal in 1888, but Hepburn was subsequently re-employed, first as Professor in the English Department and ultimately as Dean of the College of Liberal Arts. (Today we call it the College of Arts and Science). The outcome seemed to reflect the opinion of the trustees that while both had caused the conflict, Hepburn was less offensive than McFarland. At any rate, they had to search for a new president to take the place of McFarland. The successor would be a young man dramatically different from the grizzled old veterans who had returned to campus in 1885 to start the New Miami on its way.

The new president had the unlikely name of Ethelbert Dudley Warfield, but he was eager to begin his duties at only twenty-seven years of age—so young he had to grow a bushy black beard to seem older than he was. A graduate of Princeton, Warfield had done advanced study at Oxford University in England, and then had earned a degree in law at Columbia University. When he agreed to become president of Miami University, he also agreed to instruct courses in history and political science. He did so for the three years he headed Miami, from 1888 to 1891. He was 6' 4" tall, handsome, well-mannered, a cosmopolitan from the East who moved in the highest circles of New York society, and he brought with him a faculty much like himself—young men, mostly in their twenties, graduates of Eastern universities.

This new faculty would soon be styled the "Dude Faculty" by the presidents of the neighboring women's colleges of Oxford. They were bachelors when they came, but four of them in three short years took wives from the Western Seminary faculty. Warfield had taken bachelor's quarters on Church Street when he arrived, with a butler and a cook in attendance, and he spent much time in Cincinnati, where he was welcomed into the select social circle of the Tafts, the Herrons, and the Longworths, leaders of Queen City society. He and his fellow faculty members also made a point of spending their entire summers away from Oxford, primarily to travel in Europe. A new style was set for the Miami administration and faculty by the new President and his colleagues who were graduates of Princeton, Yale, Amherst, and MIT.

There were seven of them altogether, and one of their innovations in the fall of 1888, on their arrival in Oxford, was the introduction of a new sport, football. At the time, football was regarded as an Eastern sport, because Princeton had been one of the first two American colleges to play football. The very first intercollegiate football game had been played in New Jersey between Princeton and Rutgers. Among the four Princetonians on the New Miami faculty was one of the football heroes of Princeton University, a young man well-known in the late nineteenth century, named Marc Parrott.

Marc Parrott came to teach in the preparatory school on the Miami campus, but later, he would be renowned as a Shakespearean scholar, though at Princeton he had starred in football. Another football player on the faculty was Walter Ray Bridgman, nicknamed Jim Bridgman, who had starred on the team at Yale. They took the lead, and with the encouragement of the president, the Miami campus soon was alive with the sights and sounds of passing and kicking and running and the cheers of Miami undergraduates infatuated with the new sport.

A Miami football team was soon organized and a challenge was issued to the nearest college, the University of Cincinnati, to form a team and schedule a game. The Dude Faculty all proposed to play, since at that time there were no rules or restrictions to prevent faculty and students from playing football together. Miami counted on having a distinct advantage over the Cincinnati squad because of their experienced faculty, with stars such as Parrott and Bridgman. However its team averaged 140 pounds in weight—decidedly underweight for a varsity football team today, since many on the current Miami team would be nearly twice the size of the Miami team of 1888. Even with the faculty participating, 140 pounds was the average weight of the Miami football team. Cincinnati accepted the challenge and fielded a team much bigger than the Miami boys, easily outweighing them by averaging 160 pounds.

The time selected for the first intercollegiate football game in Ohio, and one of the first west of the Allegheny Mountains, was December 8, 1888. Most college football games today are played in September and October, because the weather is usually too cold in November and almost always too cold in December. The first game was played in a freezing rain, colder than snow. Furthermore, just a week before the big game, the Miami squad suffered a real loss. President Warfield, who had every intention of playing in the big game, was tackled by an overly exuberant sophomore in scrimmage and injured his knee so badly he had to drop out. President Warfield was asked instead to be the referee; he was perhaps the reason why the game was not as one-sided as it might have been: the final score was 0-0. Since 1888, more than 100 games have been played by Miami and Cincinnati, in what has turned out to be the longest lasting intercollegiate football rivalry west of the Alleghenies, and in that long-standing rivalry, Miami has won more games than it has lost.

I remember a call I received shortly after I came to Miami as President in 1965. The caller was a gentleman in New York City named Clarence Dickinson, who identified himself as a member of the Miami squad in the first Miami-Cincinnati game in 1888. He wanted me to know that he would be with us in spirit if not in body for the annual football game against Cincinnati, and he wished the team well. It was 1965 and he had played in 1888—77 years earlier.

So, in the fall of 1888, as the New Miami was just beginning, the new sport of football was introduced, and the game was played in the middle of the campus, in an area of lawn that was reasonably clear of shrubbery, flowers, and tree stumps. Today, that area is surrounded by buildings: Harrison Hall, King Library, Bishop Hall, Alumni Hall, and Elliott and Stoddard Halls. The campus, not a football field, was the site of the first football game played in Ohio.

In 1888 there was a New Miami, a new sport, and a new student body: women had been admitted for the first time. The former president, Robert White McFarland, had favored co-education because he was eager to enter his own daughter, Frances, as a female student. He succeeded, because in 1887, the year before he left, his daughter was one of five women who enrolled at Miami. For a long time it was thought that the first female student allowed to enroll at Miami was Ella McSurely, in the fall of 1888. But Frances McClure, when she was working in the Special Collections Room of the Library, came upon an earlier registration book, which clearly showed the handwritten names of five female students who entered Miami in the fall of 1887, and the first name was that of Frances ("Fanny") McFarland. It was Fanny McFarland who would later marry Llewellyn Bonham, and they would come to live in the house that President Stanton had built on Spring Street, once the Stanton House but now the Bonham House.

Frances McFarland's name was followed by a second name prominent in the history of Oxford, Daisy McCullough. She is remembered today as the benefactress of the McCullough-Hyde Hospital on Church and

Poplar Streets. Daisy McCullough would live for many years on High Street, in a home that was once one of the show-places of Oxford, but is today shrouded by bushes. It stands next to the Beta Theta Pi Chapter House on one side, and the Lottie Moon House on the other side. The house looks very different today, but Daisy McCullough once lived there, and she was the second female student to enroll at Miami in October of 1887, just after Frances McFarland.

Why is Ella McSurely usually credited with being the first woman student at Miami? First of all, President McFarland probably did not want to publicize the fact that his daughter had been allowed to enroll in what had been an all-male college, since co-education was still controversial in 1887. Ella McSurely, on the other hand, had no reason for concealing the fact that she began her course of studies in 1888, and that subsequently she was awarded a baccalaureate degree in 1901. She eventually became a librarian at Miami, since her father, William G. McSurely, had been on the board of trustees and then had become head librarian. Ella worked for her father, and she served as a librarian for many years at Miami. The word spread that she was the first woman student, and she did not disclaim the honor later. Indeed, her obituary speaks of Ella McSurely as the first woman student at Miami, and it has been on record for a long time.

It is easy to see how such claims may be made to honor the dead; for instance, there is the tombstone of George Junkin, the second president of Miami, in Stonewall Jackson Cemetery in Lexington, Virginia. Carved in stone, and therefore beyond question, is the message that George Junkin was the president and founder of Lafayette College and Miami University. Anyone reading the tombstone would be likely to take it as fact that Dr. Junkin was responsible for starting Miami, when the truth is that he was the successor rather briefly of a more popular president, Robert Hamilton Bishop.

So with the coming of the Dude Faculty to Miami in 1888, there was an open welcome for women students. That was true at any rate of the younger faculty members; only the old curmudgeon, Dr. Hepburn, continued to believe that it was a mistake to bring women to the campus and award degrees to them. He would carry that belief to his grave, but in spite of his presence Miami became co-educational in the late 1880s. It was less easily accepted off campus, where the foes of co-education at Miami were quickly evident. Foremost among them was the president of the Oxford College for Women, Lafayette Walker, nicknamed "Faye" Walker. His reason for outspokenly condemning the admission of women to Miami was that he saw the handwriting on the wall for his own institution. To him, the day Miami began admitting women was the beginning of the end for separate women's colleges in Oxford. And he was right. In 1928, Oxford College became part of Miami; in 1974 the Western College for Women became part of Miami. There was at one time, a third institution, the Oxford Female College, but it had already become part of the Oxford College for Women in 1867.

The New Miami was soon to have a further distinction, beyond football and co-education. For leading one of the two major parties in the United States presidential election of 1888 was a Miami graduate, Benjamin Harrison, of the class of 1852. At his side was his wife, future First Lady Caroline Scott Harrison, daughter of Professor and Mrs. John Witherspoon Scott, who had been born in Oxford in 1832 in the Scott House at the corner of Campus and High. To make it more exciting for people at Miami and in Oxford, the campaign manager for Benjamin Harrison's opponent, Grover Cleveland of New York, was Calvin Brice, class of 1863, a railroad magnate and principal benefactor of the New Miami. So the head of one presidential ticket and the campaign manager for the other were graduates of the same university. There was immense excitement on campus and in town on the night of the election, and a great thrill as the returns began to come in, showing Benjamin Harrison as the likely winner. The final outcome was in doubt until early morning, because Benjamin Harrison did not win the majority of the popular vote, but he won the vote in the electoral college, since he won the majority of states that had the largest blocks of electoral votes. It was a historic moment for the American political system, for though Harrison lost the election by 100,000 popular votes, he easily won the election in the electoral college, and became 23rd President of the United States.

The Harrison presidency is remembered for the entry into the Union of six new states, most of them in the northwest, the annexation of the territory of Hawaii, and the resolution of certain boundary disputes with our neighbors through the intercession of our State Department. Harrison had a reasonably successful administration, and in 1892, the Republicans nominated him for a second term in the White House. He would again be opposed by Calvin Brice, fellow Miamian, who sought the Democratic nomination in 1892 only to lose it to Grover Cleveland, who had been Democratic nominee for President in three consecutive elections—1884, 1888, and 1892. What made the election of 1892 even more exciting at Miami was the fact that the vice-presidential candidate at the side of Benjamin Harrison was another Miamian, Whitelaw Reid, class of 1855. Reid, from Xenia, Ohio, was at this time the editor and publisher of the *New York Tribune.* It would be the only time in American political history that the candidates for President and Vice President, put forward by a major political party, were graduates of the same college, even if they were not destined to win the election.

The New Miami was also blessed in the fall of 1888

with a major gift from one of the nationally prominent political leaders, railroad builder Calvin Brice. He had earlier given funds to help pay off the indebtedness remaining from the Civil War years, and to establish two endowed professorships, but now he saw the need for a new science building on campus. The old one-room, one-story building nicknamed Old Egypt would be replaced, when Calvin Brice matched the $15,000 grant from the State of Ohio with a gift of $15,500 to construct a science building that would have the appropriate name of Brice Hall. It was built in 1890 and 1891, and located just off Slant Walk.

As it turned out, Brice Hall was built in the last years of the brief administration of President Warfield. Warfield's presidency was brief, because he came under increasing criticism for all the changes and innovations that were taking place on the Miami campus, including the return of compulsory chapel.

Robert White McFarland, the first layman to be President of Miami, had seen to it that chapel ceased to be required, but Warfield, another layman, saw wisdom in its restoration. The return to compulsory chapel by President Warfield outraged McFarland's supporters, who were still numerous in town. Warfield was also under fire for supporting co-education, and his most outspoken critic was the President of Oxford College, Lafayette Walker. Faye Walker became increasingly vocal in his criticism of Warfield, adding to it the charge that he and his Dude Faculty were spending too much time in the capitals of Europe or hobnobbing with the Tafts, the Herrons, and the Longworths in Cincinnati. Part of the criticism reflected the belief that Miami should be recruiting more students from the immediate region around Oxford, especially from the sons and daughters of local farmers. Faye Walker spoke scornfully in public of the Easterners who were now in charge of Miami. In 1890, Warfield was offered the presidency of the Ohio State University, but declined. Then in 1891, he was offered the presidency of Lafayette College in eastern Pennsylvania, and he accepted. With him went most of the Dude Faculty—all but one, Professor Roger Johnson, Professor of Philosophy, one of the four Princeton graduates brought in by Warfield. But Miami University had become a different institution under Warfield, emphasizing the sciences, co-education, and football, each of which would play an increasing role in the New Miami.

When President Warfield tendered his resignation, pressure was brought to bear on the Miami University Board of Trustees to replace him with someone from the Midwest or the West, since the sophisticated Easterners that had been members of the faculty were resented by many local people. The new president did come from the West, from Colorado, where he had been president of Longmont College for Women in the foothills of the Rocky Mountains, and his name was William Oxley Thompson. President Thompson served from 1891 to 1899, continuing in those eight years some of the directions set by Warfield, but making some alterations of his own. Under President Thompson, the new Brice Hall was completed and a new Bachelor of Science degree was instituted. Until then, only one degree, the Bachelor of Arts, could be earned at Miami, but the Bachelor of Science degree would be available after 1893. President Thompson also favored athletics, and in his administration, the first Miami gymnasium was completed in 1896, named the Herron Gym in honor of the Chairman of the Board of Trustees, John Herron of Cincinnati, father-in-law of William Howard Taft. And in the Thompson years, the first Miami football field was constructed at the corner of Patterson and High, to be known as the Miami Field from the middle 1890s until it was closed in 1982, making way for the newer and larger Yager Stadium on Bonham Road.

CHAPTER X

MIAMI MOVES FROM EAST TO WEST

Presidents Warfield and Thompson were distinctly different types. Warfield was young, came from the East, was a graduate of Princeton, and all the faculty he hired were from the same section of the country. The Dude Faculty were sophisticated, polished, socially adept. In contrast, Thompson came from the West, from Colorado, and was a decade older than the man he replaced. He was able to go out and talk to the farmers of southwestern Ohio in a language they understood, and he could easily recruit their sons as Miami students. Many felt that Warfield and his Dude Faculty were too much Easterners who could not talk to farmers, but Thompson had been born on a farm in Muskingum County, had graduated from Muskingum College before he went west, and seemed the right man for the Miami presidency.

Thompson had come to Oxford from Longmont College in Colorado, a Presbyterian college where he had simultaneously served as president and as the minister of the local congregation. He had been twice widowed, since his first wife died in childbirth and his second after an illness, and he came back to Ohio to be among the people he knew best, farmers like himself. As Miami president from 1891 to 1899, he vigorously recruited students from the farms of southwestern Ohio, bringing to campus a number of talented young men from local families, some of whom would stay on or return to campus after graduation as distinguished leaders. Two of them became Miami presidents, Raymond Mollyneaux Hughes from 1911 to 1927, and Alfred H. Upham from 1928 to 1945. But, in spite of his best efforts, the enrollment at Miami never passed 200, and it was usually 110, 120, or 130 in the course of the 1890s, mostly male. Thompson recruited a few female students, but the female enrollment never passed 16 in his eight years at the helm.

Thompson responded to the criticisms that had been directed against Warfield, and found a way to speak to the people of the region that brought new students to campus. However, the results of his recruiting efforts were meager, except for the two later presidents, Hughes and Upham. He had greater success in emphasizing the sciences, helped by the gift from Calvin Brice, which enabled Miami to build Brice Hall, providing classrooms and laboratories for scientific subjects such as chemistry, physics, biology, and geology.

Old Egypt had been the only science building until Brice Hall was built, and in 1898 it was finally torn down, replaced by Brice Hall as a new building properly equipped for scientific study. Brice Hall, built in 1891 at a cost of $30,500, half from the State of Ohio and half from the gift of Calvin Brice, contained the latest and best scientific apparatus needed for the instruction of undergraduate students. And Miami now could offer two degrees, the Bachelor of Science as well as the Bachelor of Arts.

In addition to fostering the sciences at Miami, Thompson also fostered physical education and intercollegiate athletic competition, since he was a firm believer in developing both the body and the mind. He was himself a big, rugged individual, always physically fit, and he wanted students to train their bodies as they were training their minds. Thompson built the first gymnasium in the university's history, since until his presidency Miami had no more than a room in Old Main with some exercise equipment, hardly enough to support a program of physical training for students.

The gym that Thompson built in 1896 was a gymnasium with a full basketball court on the second floor, a running track halfway up the wall around the basketball court, and offices as well as physical education classrooms on the first floor. It was called Herron Gym in honor of the Chairman of the Board of Trustees, John W. Herron of Cincinnati, father-in-law of William Howard Taft, and stood on the site of the present parking lot near Roudebush Hall. It stayed there from 1896 until its demolition in 1983, its name having been changed in the interim to Van Voorhis Hall, in honor of Tom Van Voorhis, a physical education instructor, coach, and athletic director in the 1920s, 1930s, and 1940s. The building had outlived its usefulness by the time it was torn down, and it was handsomely replaced, in part by Millett Hall, and in part by the present Recreation Center located on the south campus, the two together providing Miami with far larger and better space for indoor sports.

The old gym had a basketball court which seated only 500 spectators, and a running track halfway up the wall that took runners 22 laps to cover a mile, forcing those who used it to move around in small tight circles. It was as inadequate as the swimming pool at Sawyer Gymnasium on the Western campus, which had to be converted into a storage building. Sawyer pool was great for practicing turns, since once you plunged in you swam two strokes and were ready to swim back, but it was not much good for anything else.

The old Herron Gym became Van Voorhis Hall in time, and continued to be used for basketball, but only for intramural competition. On its first floor, the offices of the Air Force ROTC were installed, and when I came to Miami in 1965, I can remember standing in the office of Air Force Colonel H.P.G.H. Thomas, trying to talk to him while a game was being played overhead. All we could hear was the basketball being dribbled down the court, causing the wooden floor to vibrate: you'd hear thump, thump, thump, swish; thump, thump, thump, swish. As the ball bounced, the chandeliers in the first floor offices swung back and forth. But Herron gym was at least a beginning for indoor sports at Miami; outdoor sports like football and track had their facilities on Miami Field. The old Miami Field was located at the corner of Patterson and High, (where the Pearson Hall Biological Sciences Building stands today), with a quarter-mile cinder track around a football field in the center.

The first football game, between Miami and Cincinnati in 1888, had been played in the center of campus, but by 1896 Miami Field was providing a new facility on the corner of Patterson and High Streets. I can remember meeting an alumnus who had played in the first football game on that field, Augustus—better known as "Gus" —Kumler, who had played in 1896 in the first football game on Miami Field. The Kumler family is remembered for donating funds to build a chapel which still stands on the campus of Western College for Women. Gus Kumler came to campus in the 1970s for his 75th reunion, the lone survivor of his class, and reminisced about the games he had played on Miami Field. He still agreed with Dr. Hepburn that Miami would have been better off as an all-male school. Gus was 102 years of age when he came to the campus for the last time, to watch a Miami vs. Central Michigan basketball game. At the half, he was invited out on court, and he took the microphone, spoke to the crowd, then went into a little dance, to the delight of the spectators, who couldn't believe that a 102-year-old man could do such a thing. He did, even though he never made it to 103.

From 1896 until 1983, all football games and track meets were held on Miami Field. In 1983, when it was replaced by the new Yager Stadium at the extreme north end of campus, there was only one football field in the entire nation which was older than Miami Field: Franklin Field in Philadelphia, used by the University of Pennsylvania since 1895, which was one year older than

Miami Field. The last football game played at Miami Field was in November of 1982; since then every home game has been played at Yager Stadium.

William Oxley Thompson, a firm believer in physical education and intercollegiate athletics, left Miami in 1899, the 75th year since classes had begun in 1824, to go to Ohio State, where he served as president for the next quarter of a century. At Ohio State, he had ample opportunity to encourage physical education and intercollegiate athletic competition, helping Ohio State emerge as one of the nation's foremost athletic powers. The Ohio Stadium, still in use in Columbus, is William Oxley Thompson's legacy in the middle of the Ohio State campus.

When Thompson left to go to Ohio State in 1899, his place was taken by a Miami graduate, David Stanton Tappan, class of 1864. Warfield had been the youngest Miami president in his mid-twenties, Thompson still a young man in his mid-thirties, but Tappan came in 1899 when he was fifty-five years of age, with a family of eight children, after having served as minister in a succession of Presbyterian churches. He was the last of nine Presbyterian ministers who served as president of Miami, and his administration lasted only three years. But during his time as president, Miami graduated its first women students, conferring baccalaureate degrees on three women in the spring commencement of 1900. Until then, all female students had been enrolled as special students, none working toward a degree, but with Dr. Tappan's coming, the baccalaureate was finally conferred on women. It is appropriate that today a residence hall in the south quad bears the name of Tappan, and it is a hall for freshman women.

The conferring of the first baccalaureate degrees on women came in the spring of 1900 and was a happy event on campus. That fall, however, tragedy struck, with the outbreak of typhoid fever which devastated Miami students and Oxford townspeople. The cause, strangely enough, was the installation of indoor plumbing, including toilet facilities, in Old Main, the principal academic building on campus. It is hard to believe that until 1900 Miami still had privies on campus, but there they were, wooden and smelly, until they were replaced with indoor plumbing. Unfortunately, these new facilities in the west wing of the Old Main building were not so advanced in discharging and treating sewage as to avoid the risk of epidemics. There was a spring near Old Main which afforded hundreds of gallons of fresh, pure, cold drinking water every hour. Everyone came to drink and enjoy the good cold, clear spring water. But the spring was too close to the west wing of Old Main to avoid the contamination of effluents from the new indoor plumbing system, and the result was that typhoid fever broke out in the fall of 1900. Two Miami students died, several townspeople died, and among the victims was Lucy Tappan, one of President Tappan's eight children. She was said by those who knew the President to be his favorite daughter, and with her death, President Tappan went into deep mourning. His grief was so profound that in the fall of 1901 he announced his intention to leave at end of that academic year. When he departed in 1903, he was the last Presbyterian minister to serve as Miami President.

Miami did, however, have one more clergyman as president, since Tappan's return to the role of Presbyterian minister brought to the campus the first and only Methodist minister to serve as president. His name was Guy Potter Benton and he was Ohio-born, but he had received his undergraduate education at Baker University in Kansas. He had taught in a number of schools in Kansas and Iowa before becoming president of Upper Iowa University in 1902, a Methodist church school then and now. Like Presidents Warfield and Thompson, President Benton would teach history and political science at Miami, since he had taught those subjects at both the secondary and college levels before coming to Miami in 1902. He was short and stocky in build, but had an exceptional speaking voice, which could reach thousands without amplification, and he was blessed with a personal charisma that endeared him quickly both to the campus and the town. In his nine years as Miami president, from 1902 to 1911, Guy Potter Benton became one of Miami's most popular leaders. He loved students and they loved him, and he was the first president to live in Lewis Place, now the presidential home on High Street overlooking the campus.

He would also be the first president affected by a very significant act of the Ohio General Assembly, a bill introduced in March 1902, by Charles Seese of Akron, calling for the establishment of professional teacher training institutions at both Athens and Oxford. In 1902, when the Seese Bill was put into the hopper, Ohio was one of the last five states and territories without state support for the professional preparation of teachers, the others being Wyoming, Delaware, Alaska, and Hawaii. Teachers at that time in Ohio came from out-of-state as well as in-state schools, but they were educated on private college campuses, since Ohio had appropriated no money for teacher education. Public support for teacher preparation came from local municipalities and counties, not from the state itself. All teacher preparation in the late nineteenth and early twentieth centuries was called "Normal." Normal education simply meant teacher education, and most states had Normal schools, but Ohio had only City Normals and County Normals as well as summer institutes, no state Normal schools. To meet the demand for new teachers, it was typical at the time to take the biggest boy out of the spring graduating class and make him a teacher in the fall.

I am speaking from experience, because my father was the biggest boy in his graduating class in 1903. At the age of 18, he became a teacher in a one-room country school in Ashland County, Ohio. He had played football at Savannah Academy, and since he was the biggest football player on the team, he was tapped to be a teacher. In the vernacular of that time, he was appointed because he could handle the students: the first requisite for a teacher then was to be able to handle the students. If you were big and strong, you could handle them, and so my father taught school for six years before he finally had enough money to go to college. There, he learned about the subjects he was supposed to be teaching to the students he knew how to handle. In all, he taught for forty-nine years, going from a one-room country school to the Cleveland public schools. The old formula had worked, but not very well, and the ones who suffered most from it were the students.

So Representative Seese sponsored a bill that would establish Normal colleges or teacher training programs in Ohio, at two established colleges in Athens and Oxford. The bill called for the two colleges to become known as the Ohio State Normal College of Ohio University and the Ohio State Normal College of Miami University. The results were what we know today as schools of education. At Miami, we call ours the School of Education and Allied Professions. When Normal Colleges were first established, they offered two-year certification. Not until the 1920s would the baccalaureate degree come to be a principal objective of professional teacher programs, and even as late as the 1950s, there were certified teachers in the classrooms of some Ohio schools who had never gotten their baccalaureate but had only a two-year certificate.

I remember the first commencement I attended at Kent State University in 1947, when my own aunt, who had been a certified teacher for twenty years, received her baccalaureate degree. The establishment of Normal Colleges led to rapid growth at Ohio University and Miami University, which had been quite small but now suddenly had an influx of aspiring teachers, particularly of women, dramatically increasing their student numbers. In 1902, when Guy Potter Benton came to Miami as President, the Seese Bill was newly passed, and Miami enrolled 207 students that fall, 78 of them women. Two years later, in 1904, total enrollment was 319, surpassing for the first time the old record enrollment of 266 in 1855, just before the Civil War. Ninety-eight women were among the 319 students, and by 1905, when enrollment was 419, 187 were women. Miami kept growing by leaps and bounds, going from 433 in 1906, with 197 women, to 444 in 1907, with 227 women. In 1911, the last year of the Benton administration, Miami had reached a total enrollment of 700, of whom 330 were women. For its first century, Miami had a maximum of 266 students, but by the end of the first decade of the twentieth century, enrollment had ballooned to 700 students, a dramatic increase.

The increase in students called for an increase in faculty. When Benton began as president, there were 13 on the Miami faculty; when he left in 1911, there were 39. There had been professors of science when he came; when he left, there were professors of chemistry, biology, physics, and geology. The larger faculty led to departmentalization, so that, rather than having one professor for all the sciences, professors would be hired to teach only chemistry, or biology, or physics, or geology.

The same thing happened in the social sciences, where by 1911, Miami had departments of history, government (later political science), sociology, and geography. There was also the beginning of academic divisions. Throughout the nineteenth century, there had been only one division, liberal arts, which encompassed all fields and all students. After 1902, there were two divisions, liberal arts (now called Arts and Science), and education, first called the Ohio State Normal College, later the School of Education and Allied Professions. The coming of divisions meant the appointment of deans for the first time. Whereas there had been one central administrator, the president, who was also a full-time faculty member, now there would be deans heading the academic divisions. The first dean of the new college of education, or Ohio State Normal, was F.B. Dyer, who stayed only a year, 1902-03, and was replaced by Harvey C. Minnich, who had been superintendent of schools in Middletown. Harvey Minnich was really the founding Dean of Education at Miami, because he continued in the new post from 1903 through the 1920s, and left a lasting mark on the university.

With the appointment of a Dean of Education, Miami needed to appoint a Dean of Liberal Arts, and it appointed Andrew Dousa Hepburn, who had come to the campus in 1868 as the first Professor of English, then had been promoted to President of the Old Miami before the Civil War, left to become president of Davidson College in North Carolina, and returned to the New Miami, where, in 1902, he was named the first Dean of Liberal Arts. He served in that capacity for six years, until 1908.

To the existing academic deans in two divisions, Miami added personnel deans. In 1905, the first Dean of Women was appointed to look after 187 women on campus; she was Elizabeth Hamilton, a graduate of the Oxford College for Women. She served as Miami's Dean of Women from 1905 until her retirement forty years later in 1945. Miami today has a Hamilton Hall and a Minnich Hall quite close together, named for the Dean of Women and the Dean of Education in the early part of the twentieth century. I can remember that when I came to Miami in 1965, Miss Hamilton had retired but was still living with her sister at a place called Kittery Point, Maine. Kittery Point was on the extreme eastern coast of Maine, and we did not see her, but for the first several years in Oxford, we used to get a Christmas card from Dean Elizabeth Hamilton, always expressing best wishes for the faculty, the staff, and the student body of Miami.

Because of the increasing presence of women on campus, the first sorority was established at Miami in 1902. Miami had already gained a national reputation as "Mother of Fraternities," and with a total of 78 women on campus, it was appropriate for it to have sororities as well. The sorority founded at Miami was Delta Zeta, and its national headquarters and museum today stand at the corner of Campus and Church in Oxford.

Also, with the coming of the Ohio State Normal College, Miami would enroll its first African-American students. Miami was now not only co-educational, as it had been since 1887, but in 1902, with the passage of the Seese Bill, the university became bi-racial as well. The first African-American student to be admitted to Miami was Nellie Craig, a native of Oxford, who was admitted to the new teacher preparation program in the Normal College. In 1905, she completed her course of study and received her certificate. She taught school in the Cleveland area for a number of years, and married a Cleveland man who was also a strong educator and a firm supporter of the university. His name was J.M. Walker. A second African-American student, Lametta Granger, was admitted in 1903, also from Oxford. She taught in southwestern Ohio schools and eventually married John T. Mann of Xenia.

Since it was now increasingly co-educational, Miami needed a residence hall for women. There were two historic residence halls for men, Elliott Hall built in 1828 and Stoddard Hall built in 1835. The first women's residence hall was constructed in 1905 and misnamed Hepburn Hall, honoring the man who had said that only over his dead body would there be women at Miami. He was still living when the first women's residence hall was named in his honor, but the old Hepburn Hall no longer stands. Instead, there is a new Hepburn Hall in the north quad, while the site of old Hepburn Hall has become a plaza of lawn, sidewalks, and bicycle racks in front of King Library. Hepburn Hall, later to be named Clokey Hall in the 1960s, had to be demolished when King Library was built, since the architectural plan called for the front porch of King to be built where the back porch of the old Hepburn Hall stood. The two buildings were merged for a time in 1968, when the first phase of King Library was nearing completion and the back porch of old Hepburn Hall was torn off.

One night in 1968, I was having dinner with my wife in Lewis Place when we were suddenly disturbed by a frantic pounding on the front door. I rushed to open the door, and found three women students standing there. They were breathless and asked me to come quickly, because workmen razing old Hepburn Hall had just opened the cornerstone. The wrecker's ball had smashed into it and struck a copper box inside, spilling the contents all over the grass. I thanked them for telling me, and followed them as they ran to the campus. When I got to the wrecking site, I saw the copper box and its contents dumped on the grass. I examined them, and discovered a copy of the Oxford newspaper printed on the day in 1905 when the copper box had been placed in the cornerstone of Hepburn Hall. I opened the paper, and immediately my eye caught the name of W.J. Meyer, grocer, the father of "Bang" Meyer. To generations of Miami students, the name Bang Meyer had meant a great deal as the man who sold late-night snacks on campus. He was a real character in Oxford, who later ran what he called the Junction House on College Corner Pike, an old building surrounded by acres of unkempt lawn and the remnants of cabins that once served as overnight accommodations before motels came to town.

In the copper box along with the newspaper were a catalog of Miami University for 1905-1906, and some leaflets announcing current programs in liberal arts and education. There were coins—pennies, dimes, quarters, nickels—and some dollar bills. And then my eye caught a little black notebook with two ribbons streaming from it, in old rose and green, the ribbons of Delta Zeta sorority. I opened up the notebook and read the names of Delta Zetas in 1902, 1903, 1904, and 1905. Then my eye fell upon an envelope with the signature of Andrew Dousa Hepburn, for whom the newly built hall was being named. And I thought to myself, at long last, I'm going to see what the old curmudgeon thought about the great honor of having the first women's residence hall at Miami named for him. I opened the envelope, took out three sheets of paper, and I looked at the first sheet. I couldn't believe it. It was blank. Well, I thought, Dr. Hepburn had three sheets of paper and wasted one, but there were two more. The second sheet was also blank, and so was the third. I was amazed that Professor-turned-President-turned-Dean Hepburn had missed this golden opportunity for acknowledging the honor of having a women's residence hall named for him. But then I thought to myself: "Wait a minute. He just did it. He couldn't think of one thing to say that was positive. He had been asked to write a letter for posterity to be put in the copper box and sealed in the cornerstone, and he apparently concluded that it would be a long time in the future, long after he was gone, before that copper box would be opened, so he put three blank pieces of paper in an envelope and signed it, for me to read in 1968." The old Hepburn Hall, built as the first women's residence hall in 1905, was finally demolished in 1968; fortunately, the new Hepburn Hall built in the north quad is a hall for men.

Among the changes that occurred with the coming of the Normal College in 1902 was the prohibition of the sale of liquor in the town of Oxford. For years, the principal mainline churches had been fighting to end the sale of intoxicants in the Oxford groceries. In 1905, with an enrollment of 187 women students at Miami, the town finally agreed that the time had come to support prohibition. In the fall of 1905, voters chose to outlaw the sale of beer and wine, and prohibition would remain in effect for the next 75 years. Oxford was a dry town from 1905 until 1980, though the sale of beer with what was called a non-intoxicating alcoholic content of 3.2% or less was permitted. Naturally, 3.2 beer was sold in prodigious quantities in Oxford, particularly after World War II when the veterans returned to the campus. Oxford, in fact, came to be called the 3.2 capital of the world. People drank 3.2 beer all day and all night until 1980, and intoxication was unheard of—there was just a twinkle in the eye and a feeling of liquid saturation. But in 1980, the 75-year drought came to an end. The argument in support of repeal, "If you're old enough to fight, you're old enough to vote," finally won, and 18-year-olds who had gone to the military service and returned to campus were clearly old enough to vote prohibition away.

A constitutional amendment in the 1970s had lowered the voting age in the United States from 21 to 18, and the Miami student body that had been previously disenfranchised now had the vote. A cartoonist graphically demonstrated this change by drawing the population of Oxford as a long snake with an enormous bulge in the middle, as if a python had swallowed a rhinoceros. The population of Oxford had been constant for many years, but by 1980, the students outnumbered the townspeople by a ratio of 4 1/2 to 1, and when they went to the polls, they voted overwhelmingly to end seventy-five years of prohibition. There was one student precinct in town with no year-round inhabitants, only fraternity or residence hall occupants. It voted by a majority of 92.5% to end prohibition.

Chapter XI

THE BENTON ERA: MIAMI CENTENNIAL

Certainly one of the defining moments of Miami history came in March 1902, when the Seese Bill was enacted by the legislature of the State of Ohio. The Bill mandated two new teacher preparation schools in the state, one in Athens, one in Oxford, to be called Ohio State Normal Colleges. These have today become schools of education at both Ohio and Miami, new academic divisions which came into being in the fall of 1902. With them came a number of changes in the university, the first and most obvious of which was an increase in enrollment. Miami had never enrolled more than 200 students at any time since the close of the Civil War. In 1902, Miami enrolled 207 students, and of these, 78 were women—a notable change, for no more than 16 women had attended Miami at any time since co-education was introduced in 1887.

So, after 1902, there was a rapid increase in total students and in women students. During Guy Potter Benton's presidency, from 1902 to 1911, total student enrollment increased from 207 to 700 students, and women from 78 to 330. With growing numbers of women, security on campus needed to be improved, and the first measure was the legal prohibition of intoxicants in the town of Oxford. Prohibition of the sale of alcohol had the support of local churches and the university, and in 1905 it was voted in, making Oxford a dry community for the next 75 years, from 1905 to 1980, when repeal was finally approved with the help of a large student vote.

With student numbers growing, faculty growth was also evident. Where there had been one professor teaching all the sciences, now there were specialists in chemistry, physics, geology, and biology. Where there had been one humanities professor before, there would now be a professor of history and a professor of English literature. It was a period of rather spectacular growth, when contrasted with the earlier Miami years, but it was almost stopped by a controversial piece of legislation, introduced in the Ohio General Assembly with the support of former Miami President William Oxley Thompson, who was serving as President of the Ohio State University.

President Thompson of Ohio State and President Benton of Miami were on opposite sides of the controversy, which began in 1906 when the Lybarger Bill was introduced on the floor of the Ohio House. The Lybarger Bill called for reduction of programs at both Ohio and Miami universities to teacher training only. Miami's whole tradition had been the liberal arts, which in the nineteenth century was the sole division of the university. Now it was proposed that a century-old tradition be discarded, and that a new program become the focus of instruction. Certificate programs lasted only two years for teachers, and so the net effect of the Lybarger Bill would have been that two years of teacher preparation would replace four years of liberal arts. Miami would become a junior college, and so would Ohio University, if the Lybarger Bill were passed. The future of both institutions was threatened, and the two presidents immediately went to Columbus and virtually camped there for two weeks, while the Lybarger Bill was under consideration by the legislature. President Alston Ellis of Ohio University and President Guy Potter Benton of Miami University called on the alumni of both schools to rally to the defense of their traditional educational programs, and the alumni responded. Because of the effective political campaign against it, the Lybarger Bill was defeated in the House after two weeks of vitriolic debate. In its stead, a new proposal was introduced that eventually did pass, known as the Eagleson Act of 1906. This act called for Miami and

Ohio Universities to continue to offer their liberal arts programs as they had traditionally done, and to continue to offer teacher preparation programs as they had been doing since 1902, but at a more advanced level, offering both baccalaureate and master's degrees in education. And, in a sop to Ohio State, the Eagleson Act called for it to become *primus inter pares,* first among Ohio colleges and universities, offering professional and doctoral programs not available at Miami and Ohio.

Ohio State, a year later, would be authorized to offer its own teacher training programs leading to certification. Then it became clear that after 1906, the older state schools of Ohio, Miami and Ohio University, would be for baccalaureate and master's degrees, while Ohio State would be for baccalaureate, master's, and doctoral degrees, as well as degrees in law and medicine. Ohio State emerged as the university with the greatest state support, but Miami and Ohio had clearly won the controversy. If the Lybarger Bill had become law, the two oldest schools in the state would have been drastically limited and their long-standing traditions as liberal arts colleges would have been shattered.

When Ellis returned to Ohio and Benton to Miami, both were hailed as heroes for having saved their schools. Former President William Oxley Thompson, however, was regarded as a traitor in Athens and Oxford, and he has never been honored by Miami with a monument or a hall in his name, nor is there ever likely to be one. There is, of course, a Thomson Hall on the Western College campus, but it is not ThomPson Hall; rather, it is Thomson Hall, and it memorializes a president of the Western College for Women who served in the 1940s. At Ohio State, on the other hand, William Oxley Thompson has been abundantly memorialized, with a larger-than-life statue in front of the William Oxley Thompson Library. It was President Thompson, in the quarter century he served Ohio State, who dramatically increased the enrollment of that school and brought its athletic program into national prominence.

In the Benton era, implementation of the Seese Act created a new division, the Normal College, or what is today the School of Education. What followed were dramatic increases in enrollment, in the size of the faculty, in diversity of curriculum, and in departmentalization. New buildings were also constructed under Guy Potter Benton, demanded by the expanding numbers of students and of faculty.

One new building was Hepburn Hall, built in 1905 to be the first women's residence hall, but there were others in the same area of the campus. There is for instance the building we now call Hall Auditorium. Known for years as the Administration Building and Auditorium, it was erected in 1908 to provide offices for the new deans. Old Main had provided classrooms and office space through the nineteenth century, but it was no longer sufficient to house the offices of the president and the several deans. Miami also needed a larger auditorium, since the chapel room on the second floor of Old Main could seat only 200 students. Chapel was still mandatory, but there was not enough room for 700 students to assemble. So today's Hall Auditorium was built, to be called the Administration Building and Auditorium until the late 1920s, and then, with President Benton's death, to be renamed Benton Hall. It remained Benton Hall until the late 1960s, when the name Benton Hall was transferred across High Street and given to the new Behavioral Science Building.

It is true that Miami has changed many of its names for buildings, sometimes more than once. Herron Gymnasium was named for John W. Herron, Chairman of the Board of Trustees, but now we call it Phillips Hall. Herron, it was discovered, believed that women should not exercise because it would make them sweat. He did not mind if they perspired a little bit, but he thought it was indecent for them to sweat. Naturally, it was impossible to have a women's physical education building named for Herron, and so it was renamed Phillips Hall, honoring Margaret Phillips, who for forty years had chaired the Women's Physical Education Department. You will notice, however, that the name Herron Hall is engraved in stone above the entrance to Phillips Hall. The trustees have since declared that names be placed on removable plaques, which can be unscrewed in the event a name becomes no longer suitable, since they recognize that it's a bit embarrassing for a name to be engraved in stone if the name is changed.

Most name changes have been occasioned by the age of a building and the prospect of its demolition. Benton Hall, now Hall Auditorium, came to be regarded in the 1960s as a building which showed its age and was in need of major renovation. When it had been constructed in 1908, it reflected the size of the student body at that time. But when Hall Auditorium was finally renovated, it was actually reduced, from 1200 seats to 700. Seats were widened and the distance between rows was increased, so that the larger students of the later twentieth century could fit into them and move more conveniently down the aisles. It was the physical size of students, not their numbers, which dictated the renovations. Building codes had also dramatically changed, mandating new arrangements for fire protection and safety. And acoustic improvements meant that new equipment must be incorporated in a building that was to be used for concerts and lectures.

When the university asked the State of Ohio for funds to renovate Hall Auditorium, the state demurred, using a formula that if it would cost 60% or more of its replacement cost to renovate a building, the building should be torn down and replaced with a new one. There was no allowance for historic preservation then, and if the rule had prevailed, Miami would have been forced to replace rather than remodel all its older buildings. In recent years, fortunately, the State of Ohio has finally recognized the importance of architectural heritage, and Miami has been able to retain much of its traditional look.

At one time, if it appeared that a building was going to have to be demolished for lack of state support to remodel it, the name of the building would be transferred to a new building. Thus, the name would be perpetuated even if the building could not be preserved. It was just such a consideration which led the trustees to transfer the name Benton Hall from the old auditorium to the new Behavioral Science Building in 1968.

At any rate, in the Benton era in 1908, a new administration building and auditorium was built, and then, in 1909, the first library building went up on campus. Until that time, the Miami library had been in rooms assigned in Old Main for a book collection. It had been necessary to add a second room, then a third room, to the library. What was needed was a free-standing library building with the capacity to grow as the book collection grew. In 1909, the Miami book collection totaled 26,700 volumes. It had been growing ever since John W. Browne, the beggar on horseback, had accepted books to support a new college in 1810. A century later, Miami had 26,700 books, less than are acquired now in a single year, since our present library acquisitions run at an average rate of 35,000 new titles every year. Miami needed a library building by 1910, but the question was, how to get it? The answer was provided by John Shaw Billings, class of 1857.

Billings is known on campus today for the old swimming pool, named Billings Natatorium. But the name is inappropriate, since John Shaw Billings as an undergraduate was a bibliophile, a lover of books, not a swimmer. He read constantly, hours on end. Confronted with the old university limit of two books a week per student, which prevailed when he was an undergraduate, he asked his friends who didn't have the same voracious appetite for reading if they would permit him to use part of their quota. Their cooperation helped to satisfy his need to read a book every night, but it still wasn't enough. So, on weekends when the library was closed, John Shaw Billings would scale the walls of Old Main, under cover of darkness, get up on the roof, then descend through the skylight into the library rooms below where he could read to his heart's content. In the wee hours of the morning, he would climb back through the skylight, cross the roof, let himself down the outer wall to the ground below, and go back to his room. He never stole any books, but he read many more than the weekly limit while he was a Miami student.

In 1857, John Shaw Billings graduated from Miami, and promptly enrolled at the Cincinnati Medical College, later to become part of the University of Cincinnati when it was incorporated in 1871. The Medical College had come into being in 1819, led by Dr. Daniel Drake, and it was the principal educator of doctors in southwest Ohio. Billings graduated with a specialty in surgery just as the Civil War broke out. He went to war as a surgeon and knew the horrors, indeed the cruelties, of surgery on the battlefield without proper anesthesia, without proper operating equipment. There is a scene at the beginning of the film, *Dances with Wolves,* which shows graphically the horrors of amputation en masse on the battlefield, when surgeons would lop off ankles, legs, and arms just to save lives. There were many waiting to be treated and only a handful of doctors, and the end result was amputation on a massive scale.

One of those battlefield surgeons in the Civil War was John Shaw Billings. He was so distressed about his experience that at war's end he determined to do something about the primitive state of surgery. He decided he would assemble all the medical knowledge he could get his hands on from all parts of the world and incorporate it in a volume of scientific medical data to be called *Materia Medica,* that is, Medical Matters. Ultimately, he amassed 16,000 pages, which he printed in 16 volumes averaging 1,000 pages a volume. It was the medical information of the entire world, garnered from the doctors of the world, never before assembled in one collection, a prodigious effort which brought Billings world acclaim because it was a long step forward in man's capacity to treat injuries, to treat wounds, to cope with disease. In recognition of his achievement, he was appointed in 1880 as Director of the United States Public Health Service. A few years later, he responded to the request from a new university in Baltimore, Maryland, called Johns Hopkins, to help establish a new medical school, and the result was one of the foremost medical schools in the nation, with one of the premiere medical programs in the world.

In 1895, John Shaw Billings was prevailed upon to accept the directorship of what would become under his leadership the largest library in the country, the New York Public Library. He soon made it one of the principal depositories of information in virtually all subjects. He was serving as director of the New York Public Library when a steel manufacturer by the name of Andrew Carnegie sought him out, and asked him to do for the world what he had done for New York City, that is, to develop a worldwide library system financed by Carnegie. Andrew Carnegie had come to the United States as a young Scottish boy with no more than a third-grade education, and had built Carnegie Steel, which would later become the United States Steel Corporation. Having amassed a considerable fortune, he wanted to use it for the benefit of the world, especially for those like himself with little formal education. He believed that public libraries were the answer, and he enlisted the support of

Billings as the foremost librarian in the world. Between them, they laid out a plan for constructing 2,811 libraries across the globe, the most ambitious building plan in history. They stipulated that English-speaking countries would be the principal beneficiaries of these libraries, and particularly the United States of America. Of the 2,811 libraries Carnegie and Billings envisioned, 2,509 would be built in the U.S.A. They would be built with Carnegie money as a challenge grant for local communities to match with contributions of their own.

The first Miami library was built in 1909 and called Alumni Library, since Carnegie's money with Billings' support had challenged Miami alumni to raise matching funds, and they did so. It served as the main library for Miami University until the construction of King Library in the 1960s and '70s, and then it became a depository for seldom-used book materials. But a new Southwest Depository was built on the Miami campus in Middletown, and so the Alumni Library has been converted into a building for the Architecture Department, including the Art and Architecture Library. Perhaps some day there will be a building on campus known as Billings Hall in recognition of John Shaw Billings' contributions to medical knowledge and to libraries the world over, and I'm not referring to a swimming pool.

Another new building completed in the Benton era, in addition to Hepburn Hall, the auditorium and administration building now known as Hall Auditorium, and the Alumni Library, was McGuffey Hall, housing the Normal College or School of Education. McGuffey Hall, appropriately named for "The Schoolmaster to the Nation," William Holmes McGuffey, has the same red brick appearance visible in the other buildings that survive from the Benton era, Hall Auditorium and Alumni Hall, since all three were constructed about the same time.

In 1910, the School of Education was fairly exploding

on campus, and it needed to have its own building, with classrooms for students majoring in teacher education, and with offices for the dean and the faculty. The McGuffey Laboratory School, which was introduced in 1910, replaced the old preparatory department, and became a new component in the training of teachers. The School of Education required budding teachers to engage in practice teaching in elementary, junior and high schools, encouraging them to observe experienced teachers and find out what students were learning in the classroom before they themselves began teaching. Pre-college instruction had been directed towards preparing students for college, but now the focus became teacher preparation, with the students placed in something like a laboratory environment. The McGuffey Lab School, as it came to be called, was installed in the new McGuffey Hall in 1910. It continued until 1968 to be located on the second and third floors of McGuffey Hall, at which time a wholly new laboratory school was built across the street. Today we know this new school simply as the Campus Avenue Building, since in 1983 the McGuffey Lab School was finally closed.

Former students of the McGuffey Lab School were dispersed through the public schools of Oxford, and the name McGuffey was transferred to the west side of town, where it became the McGuffey Foundation School, a privately supported preparatory school. Since 1983, there has been no pre-college instruction at Miami, because the last lab school in the State of Ohio, and one of the last in the nation, was finally closed. Practice teaching still is part of teacher preparation, but it is conducted in public schools across the state.

The Benton era was noted for one additional building, this one an older structure which became part of the university in 1903, Lewis Place. Lewis Place had been built as a private residence in Oxford by a merchant from

Connecticut by the name of Romeo Lewis, who moved in with his young wife, Jane. Yes, Romeo and Jane, not Romeo and Juliet. Romeo Lewis was a Connecticut Yankee who began life in New England, then moved to Florida, where he was a founder of Tallahassee, eventually the capital city of Florida. He moved from Florida to Ohio, and brought his wife Jane to Oxford, where he built a large home in anticipation of a large family. Though Romeo and Jane Lewis did have children, sadly not one of them survived infancy.

Lewis Place today includes 17 rooms and 6 baths, and is one of the larger homes in Oxford, a handsome residence in the Southern Colonial style, white frame with pillars and a spacious front porch. When Frank Lloyd Wright, perhaps the preeminent twentieth-century American architect, visited Oxford, he was asked which building in Oxford appealed to him the most, and he replied at once, "Lewis Place." He thought it singularly beautiful, and particularly praised the rear elevation of Lewis Place. It was built between 1837 and 1839, and has the antebellum look of many old Southern mansions.

The year 1837 was the year in which panic broke out, following the issuance of the Jackson Specie Circular, and for the next several years there was a marked downturn in the economy; indeed, it was called a depression. Fortunately, Lewis Place was under construction before the depression, but it was finished in the midst of the depression, and as a result it has the best lumber in the subflooring and structural supports, and the poorest lumber in the finished work around the doors and windows. Lewis Place has walnut, maple, and oak in the subflooring, but cheap pine in the trim. It reflects the changing times, and the fact that Romeo Lewis was running out of money in the depression. Nevertheless, the building stands today as a remarkably beautiful edifice. Jane Lewis became a widow in 1843 and remained in the home alone for forty years. When she passed on, she left the home to her nephew, Philip North. He did not choose to live there, and in 1903, Philip North asked the trustees of the university if they would be interested in making Lewis Place a home for Miami presidents. They agreed, and Guy Potter Benton and his family were the first to move there in 1903.

When the Shrivers moved there in 1965, I went up to the attic and found a newspaper dated 1903, left there as packing material when the Bentons moved in. Lewis Place served as the home of Miami presidents from 1903 on, but became the property of Miami only in 1929. The North family agreed to sell it to the university at a modest price, and it has been university property ever since, home to a succession of Miami presidents.

The year 1909 of the Benton era was the year when Miami University paused to honor its centennial. It had been chartered in 1809, and 100 years had gone by, so President Benton and his faculty took appropriate measures to recognize the accomplishments of the first 100 years. One such measure was the commissioning of the first history of the university by Alfred H. Upham, Professor of English, who produced a book with the title of *Old Miami, Yale of the Early West.* The book had pen and pencil illustrations, and was written in language which today seems flowery, but there is still much of interest in this book for anyone who wants to learn about Miami history.

In his history, Alfred Upham included facts that also appeared in 1909 in an article he wrote for *The Ohio Archeological and Historical Society Quarterly.* He noted that in its first 100 years, Miami had graduated 1,826 students, among whom were a President of the United States, ten governors, three cabinet officers, seven United States Senators, twenty-three Congressmen, thirty State Senators, sixty-nine State Representatives, fifty-three judges and justices, and sixty-six army officers above the rank of captain.

In addition, thirty Miami graduates had become college presidents, and seventy-six had become college professors. Miami now graduates over 3,700 in one year, and so the 1,826 graduates of the first 100 years represent about half the number who now graduate in a single year, but their record of accomplishment is extraordinary. Alfred Upham went on to show that by occupation, 327 graduates had become lawyers, 313 had become ministers, 274 had become teachers, and 122 physicians and surgeons. There were 111 graduates who had gone into business, 80 who had become farmers, 50 who had become editors and journalists, another 50 who had written at least one book, 24 engineers, 17 manufacturers, and 13 bankers. It would be hard for 1,826 graduates of any college or university to match the record of the first 100 years of Miami alumni.

The Miami Centennial, held in 1909, marked the high point in the Benton era. Two years later, in 1911, President Benton resigned to accept the presidency of the University of Vermont in Burlington. He stayed in Vermont for several years, then accepted the presidency of the University of the Philippines in Manila. Unfortunately, it was in Manila in 1927 that Guy Potter Benton contracted a rare oriental disease, and decided the time had come to return to the states to die. He came back to the home of his daughter in Minneapolis, where he died in that same year, 1927. Before his death, he asked that his remains be taken back to Oxford for burial in the Miami University Cemetery at the south end of the campus.

Miami is one of the very few universities in the country with its own cemetery. The Oxford Cemetery has a university plot within it, where there are rows of white marble headstones with the Miami seal at the top, and with the name of the faculty member, staff member, student, president, dean, trustee, athletic director, coach, whoever it might be, engraved there. It is situated on the hill south of the Alumni Center, above Peffer Park and Bull Run:

row upon row of white headstones visible on the hillside. It is highly significant that Guy Potter Benton, who had served four universities as president, asked that his body be brought back to Miami for burial.

CHAPTER XII

THE HUGHES ERA: FIRST WORLD WAR

The Benton era ended with the Miami Centennial in 1909 and the first book-length history of the university, *Old Miami, The Yale of the Early West,* written by Alfred H. Upham. Upham took justifiable pride in the accomplishment of Miami graduates during the university's first century, noting that they included a president of the United States and members of the Senate and the House of Representatives. The Miami past was distinguished enough to serve as a challenge to the Miami of the future, which would approach its Bicentennial by enrolling twice the number in one year that had graduated in its first hundred years.

Alfred Upham was Professor of English under Benton, and had in 1907 written the lyrics of the alma mater, "Old Miami," to music written by Raymond Burke, the first Miami professor of music. Benton himself, having celebrated the Miami Centennial in 1909, resigned two years later, in 1911, to accept appointment as president of the University of Vermont in Burlington. In a final letter to every graduate of Miami during his presidency, Dr. Benton asked for support of the university in the years to come, and he concluded resoundingly with "Stand by Miami, stand by Miami, stand by Miami." He loved the school and left it with regret, taking the presidency at Vermont and then at the University of the Philippines in Manila, but when he died in 1927 from a rare oriental disease, he had no doubt where he wanted to be buried. By his own wish, his remains were sent from Minnesota, where he died, to the Oxford Cemetery, where he was buried in the Miami University plot, among other presidents, as well as trustees and faculty. After his death in 1927, the trustees voted to rename the auditorium and administration building constructed during his presidency. They named it Benton Hall, and the name remained there until the 1960s, when it was moved to the Behavioral Science Building across High Street, and the building that once was called Benton was renamed Hall Auditorium.

After President Benton left Miami in 1911, there was a search for a successor, and the name that kept coming up was Raymond Mollyneaux Hughes. Hughes was then serving as Dean of the College of Liberal Arts, having replaced Andrew Dousa Hepburn on the latter's retirement in 1908. But Hughes didn't want to be president; he was fully content to remain dean and professor of chemistry. As the opening of classes approached in the fall semester of 1911, however, the trustees finally prevailed on him to become Acting President. He accepted the job with the understanding that it would be for one year only, but he found at the end of a year that the pressure was on for him to be permanent president. A national search was held, but Hughes was still the choice, and again the trustees implored him to take the job for one more year. Reluctantly, he accepted, only to find that there was even more pressure at the end of the second year for him to remain as president. Finally, he gave in, out of loyalty to his alma mater, and his presidency lasted until 1927, a total of 16 years.

In those 16 years, from 1911 to 1927, the enrollment of the university kept on growing, from 700 in 1911 to 2000 by 1927. The faculty, too, grew from 39 in 1911 to 120 by 1927. Certainly the leadership of Raymond Mollyneaux Hughes was crucial to this growth. He was a warm, kindly, thoroughly humane individual, who asserted repeatedly that the important dimension of life was not material but spiritual, and that moral values counted more than earthly riches. Because of his constant emphasis on spiritual matters, he seemed always removed from the more mundane aspects of life, and his scientific training was less evident than his religious belief.

Raymond Mollyneaux Hughes had graduated from Miami in 1893, as valedictorian of his class, already with a keen interest in the sciences. He went on to Massachusetts Institute of Technology, where he received a Ph.D. in chemistry, and was hired by his alma mater, Miami, in 1898, to replace Henry Snyder, who was Professor of Science. Hughes was also Professor of Science until the Benton years, when he was named the first Professor of Chemistry at Miami. Today, the Chemistry building is called Hughes Laboratories in his honor. Then he became Dean of the College of Liberal Arts in 1908, replacing Hepburn, and in 1911 he was named Acting President, a position he would hold for two years, until he became President in 1913 and served fourteen more years until his retirement in 1927. During the 16 years of his presidency, Hughes made a number of faculty appointments, bringing to the campus men and women of unusual competence.

Several of his key appointments deserve particular mention. First was Arthur C. Wickenden, for whom the Wickenden Lecture Series in the Department of Religion was named, now an annual lecture by a prominent professor of theology. Arthur Wickenden came to Miami first as director of the campus YMCA, until he was named by President Hughes to be the first Professor of Religion in 1923 and to head a new Department of Religion which he proposed to establish. Arthur Wickenden was a graduate of the University of Chicago, and would head the first Department of Religion on a public campus in America. Dr. Hughes wanted to insure that religion received prominence in the Humanities, in accordance with its vital role in human affairs over the course of the centuries. He asked Dr. Wickenden to avoid proselytizing for any particular religion, but to encourage student awareness of different faiths and denominations. The emphasis was to be on religion as an academic discipline, with attention to the various religions of the world. Dr. Hughes's understanding of the role of religion in the university was valid in 1923, and it is valid to this day. Within a year after Miami established the first Department of Religion on a public campus in America, the University of Iowa followed suit. In the decade following, nearly fifty more departments of religion were established, an acknowledgment that Miami had taken the right direction for public campuses in the 1920s.

Arthur Wickenden built the home on Bonham Road which is still called the Wickenden house, where he died in 1968 in his rose garden in the front yard, the house where the Shrivers now live. After he left the chair in the Department of Religion, he continued teaching the subject, and as a tribute to the man who had hired him at Miami, he wrote a biography called *Raymond Mollyneaux Hughes, Leader of Men.*

Another faculty member appointed by President Hughes was George Rider, whose name is attached today to the Miami track at the north end of campus, built as part of the Yager Stadium complex. George Rider came to Miami in 1917 as Coach Rider, with the understanding that he would coach all intercollegiate athletics and also teach physical education classes. Today Miami has coaches for each of its sports, but George Rider coached them all, and at the same time he held a teaching position on the faculty. He came from Olivet College, a church school in Michigan, not from a school noted for its athletics program, such as Ohio State or Notre Dame. But he was ready to coach football in the fall of 1917, and he was ready to coach other sports in the winter and spring. His first sport was football, and he knew that the first intercollegiate football game in the State of Ohio had been played in 1888, between Miami and Cincinnati. The Miami team had winning seasons before Coach Rider came, but not an undefeated season, and in 1917, Miami played an eight-game schedule without a loss; in its first season under Coach Rider, the Miami football team outscored the opposition by 202-0.

When the football season ended, he became the basketball coach. There had not been an undefeated season in that sport, either, but under Coach Rider, the Miami basketball team played a ten-game schedule and won all ten. It was the only undefeated team in Ohio and was conference champion that year. When basketball season ended, George Rider became the track coach. Track was his principal sport: Miami still holds the George Rider Relays for area high schools every spring and the Miami track is named for him. But Miami did not have an undefeated season in track the first year under George Rider, because it lost one meet. Still, he had done fairly well in his first year at Miami as coach of all the sports: undefeated seasons in football and basketball and only one loss in track. No wonder Miami would some day be known as "The Cradle of Coaches."

George Rider was, like President Hughes, deeply spiritual. He believed that a coach should blow the whistle at the beginning of each season and accept whoever wanted to come out for the team. He thought intercollegiate athletic competition existed to train minds as well as bodies, and his players had a deep respect for the man because of his high standards of moral as well as physical discipline. He developed a Sportsman's Code which he taught to his athletes in every sport, and he even printed it in the program for all to see. For example, in the program of the Miami vs. Ohio Wesleyan basketball game played on January 15, 1938, Coach and Director of Athletics Rider outlined his code:

A True Miami Sportsman

1. Will consider all athletic opponents as guests and treat them with all of the courtesy due friends and guests.

2. Will show respect to officials, accept adverse decisions gracefully and expect the officials to enforce the rules. Will not blame the officials for defeat.
3. Will not hiss or boo a player or official.
4. Will not utter abusive or irritating remarks from the sidelines.
5. Will not attempt to rattle an opposing player such as the pitcher in a baseball game or a player attempting to make a free throw in a basketball game.

> [When George Rider was coach, back in the 1930s and 1940s, a player from the opposing team could step to the free-throw line after a foul was called, and the crowd would be so quiet you could hear a pin drop. Contrast this behavior with that of today's fans, who shout at the free-thrower from behind the backboard so that he can't help hearing them, and who wave and hoot at him, and who may even, as I can remember on one recent occasion, just as the opposing player is about to make a shot, unfold a centerfold page from *Playboy* and hold it up for him to see while he is trying to make his free-throw.]

6. Will back his team in every honest way, but betting on the game is not necessary to show your loyalty.
7. Will applaud opponents as well as the home team when they make good plays or show good sportsmanship.
8. Will seek to win by fair and lawful means according to the spirit of the rules as well as the letter of them.
9. Will seek to win without boasting and lose without excuses.
10. Will be true to his highest ideals at all times and do nothing unworthy of a gentleman and 100% American.

He was, as the last article of his code demonstrates, a deeply patriotic individual as well as an outstanding sportsman. One of his former players, now a retired Professor of Geology, named Roy Reinhart, nicknamed "Rocky," was a track man under Coach Rider, and he can remember Coach Rider's telling his players they were not to drink Coca-Cola, because Coca-Cola contained caffeine, and caffeine was a stimulant which might give you an unfair advantage over your opponent. It was George Rider who was responsible more than any other person for establishing Miami's reputation as "The Cradle of Coaches," since he was not only a coach but a teacher of coaches.

The coaches who have made Miami famous include professionals like Weeb Ewbank and Paul Brown as well as many others, but they all attest that Coach Rider was their inspiration. One member of "The Cradle of Coaches" was Carmen Cozza, who retired after 32 years as the coach of the Yale football team. He was not only the longest-lasting coach at any Ivy League school, but also the winningest coach, with 170 victories and 8 Ivy League championships to his credit. But his proudest achievement, he was quoted as saying, was that of the 1500 football players he had coached, all but 7 had graduated. Five of them became Rhodes Scholars, and 13 became professional players, an enviable record for any coach.

President Hughes hired Arthur Wickenden to head his new Department of Religion, and George Rider to head his coaching staff and become Director of Athletics, and he hired Wallace Pattison Roudebush to be the Treasurer of Miami. Roudebush Hall, now the administration building at Miami, where the President, the Provost, and the Treasurer have their offices, was named for a graduate of the class of 1911. The Roudebush family moved to Oxford from Clermont County early in the twentieth century so that Wallace Roudebush could be educated in the preparatory school and then in the university. He graduated from Miami in 1911 as president of his class and valedictorian. Already an outstanding young leader and campus citizen, Wallace Roudebush was invited by President Hughes to join his staff immediately on graduation. He did so, and served on the staff with distinction until his death forty-five years later, in 1956.

Wallace Roudebush was first appointed to the staff in the business office, and he would be in the business office for the rest of his life, moving up to business manager, then ultimately to the position of first Vice-President for Finance and Business Affairs. It was Wallace Roudebush who instituted a number of the basic practices in the Miami business office, among them future planning. He believed in planning ahead while time was available, when money was also available to meet those future needs, so far as they could be predicted.

So, together with President Hughes in 1923, Wallace Roudebush worked out a master plan for the next century, from 1923 to 2023. Miami had an enrollment of over 1500 in 1923, and was moving quickly toward 2,000, and Roudebush and Hughes agreed that they should look ahead so that the university could meet the needs of a student body which would be significantly larger. They talked about extending the campus by acquiring farm properties before they would have to be purchased at a far higher figure. They took what in 1923 was a very liberal, very optimistic view of the university's fortunes, and predicted that by the year 2023 Miami might have a student enrollment of 5,000. Within half that time, of course, Miami would have over 16,000 students on its Oxford campus alone, but the predictions of Hughes and Roudebush seem reasonable, considering that in its first century Miami had grown from twenty to 1500 students, and that if it had doubled in its next century the enrollment would still be less than 5,000. They chose a generous figure, so they thought, in looking to the future.

Certainly Miami has benefitted from Roudebush's predictions about the rising price of farm land, since in the mid-1920s a large tract of land was purchased from the George Harvey Cook family. This land had served as the campus of one of the three colleges for women in Oxford prior to the Civil War, the Oxford Female College in the northeasternmost section of Oxford Township. After the Oxford Female College had merged with the Oxford Female Institute in 1867 to become the Oxford College for Women, it vacated its buildings and land, which remained vacant for some years until acquired by the George Cook family for conversion into a mental asylum. This facility became known as the Oxford Retreat, from 1882 until the middle 1930s, taking care of mental disorders until the middle 1920s, and then treating physical disorders until it closed in 1936. Its principal building was renamed Fisher Hall to honor Judge Elam Fisher, a trustee from Preble County north of Oxford. In 1927, after the mental patients had moved out, freshman men moved into the building, and it became a freshman dormitory until 1957. It was used as a theater for a time, then as a storage building, and finally was condemned and demolished in 1978, to be replaced by the Marcum Conference Center that today stands on its site.

The Cook family sold what would become Miami's Fisher Hall to be made into a men's dormitory, and switched its focus from the treatment of mental disorders to the treatment of physical disorders, primarily tuberculosis, for which they constructed a new building they called The Pines, known today as Wilson Hall in the east quad. The stone gateway and the curving entry drive which led to the sanitarium are still there, but Miami eventually purchased the building and renamed it Wilson Hall, in honor of Charles Ray Wilson, Acting President of Miami in 1964-65, and today it is a women's dormitory. The Cook property contained not only the sanitarium but also the Cook family residence next door, known as Cook Place, which houses the Miami board-and-room office now. What was once the Cook front yard has become Cook Field, used today for intramural sports primarily.

Miami's acquisition of this property to the east encouraged the city of Oxford to re-route the entrance to the city right up to the doorstep of Shideler Hall. Earlier, the approach to Oxford from the valley on Highway 73 had been past the stables, past the Cook home, past the Pines, and into High Street. But when the university acquired the Cook properties, Highway 73 was routed to the south, reaching the old mile square of Oxford at the front of Shideler Hall, from which traffic turns right on Patterson Avenue to High Street, and up High Street into town.

It was also under President Hughes that one of Miami's oldest traditions was introduced, Homecoming, held for the first time in 1914. Until 1914, most alumni thought of returning to campus for commencement in the spring. When President Hughes became president, he believed that in addition to the annual gathering of alumni in June, there ought to be a football weekend in the fall, when the attraction of a home football game would bring alumni back to Miami. Our opponents on the football field at that time were Ohio Wesleyan, Wittenberg, and Denison, along with the University of Cincinnati, which we began battling in 1888; Ohio University was a later opponent. But in 1914, our first homecoming game would be with the Big Red of Denison University in Granville. Miami was also known as the Big Red, so it was the Big Red vs. the Big Red. In 1914, the Big Red fought the Big Red, and the Big Red of Denison won. Homecoming was a huge success and became an annual event, which was expanded when we acquired Cook Field, to include a bonfire rally on the Friday night prior to the game. The culmination of a parade starting in the west end of town, the rally featured cheers and speeches by the coaching staff who exhorted the crowd to support the team the next day. Four years after the first homecoming game, with the support of President Hughes, several of the main thoroughfares in Oxford were paved with red bricks. And the alumni were then charged to "Follow the red brick road home to Miami." Patterson Avenue, High Street, and College Avenue all were surfaced with red bricks because of the Homecoming event.

The first Miami homecoming game was in 1914, the year World War I began. Sparked by the assassination of the heir to the Austrian throne, the Hapsburg Archduke Francis Ferdinand, in the town of Sarajevo, in the province of Bosnia, World War I pitted the Allied Nations of England and France against the Central Powers of Germany and Austria-Hungary, and President Woodrow Wilson vowed to stay out of the war. Indeed, President Woodrow Wilson was re-elected in 1916 over Charles Evans Hughes with the slogan: "He has kept us out of the war." But as it turned out, Wilson could not keep the United States out of the war, particularly when early in 1917, Germany launched an unrestricted submarine campaign against allied merchant shipping, including the ships of neutral nations such as the United States which were sending supplies to the Allies. So on April 6, 1917, President Wilson asked Congress to declare war against the Central Powers of Germany and Austria-Hungary, and America went to war.

Miami was affected by World War I, though not as much as it had been by the Civil War. A program of the federal government was installed on college campuses across the country called the Students' Army Training Corps Program. The intent of the program was to prepare young officers for future military service, though there were as yet no weapons available. Though many Miami alumni served in the American Expeditionary Force in France, students in the Army Training Corps never had to go, because the war ended before they had completed their preparation. After a year and a half of American involvement, World War I war ended on the 11th day of the 11th month of 1918, which was commemorated as Armistice Day until it was renamed Veterans' Day.

Armistice Day comes back to me when I think of my years in elementary school, junior high, and high school, because precisely at 11:00 a.m. on the 11th day of the 11th month, students would rise at their chairs and stand for a moment of silence, honoring those who gave their lives in World War I. But Miami students in the Army Training Corps were not among them. A Miami trustee named Lawrence B. "Cap" Murphy of Cincinnati had been in that Student Training Corps in the fall of 1918, and he told me once that as the war was coming to an end, Miami students nicknamed SATC the "Stick Around Till Christmas." They thought that if you waited till Christmas to be called to the Front, the war would be over first. And they were right, since Germany and Austria-Hungary surrendered to the Allies on the 11th of November. The aftermath of the war was more tragic, because peace was followed by a deadly outbreak of influenza, the worst the world has ever seen.

We lost 52,000 soldiers in World War I on the battlefield, but we lost 500,000 (nearly ten times as many) in the flu epidemic, when the war came to an end in the fall of 1918. At Miami, about half the student body and a third of the faculty came down with the flu. For six weeks, the campus was paralyzed by a raging epidemic, and neither the campus nor the town had a hospital to take care of those who were afflicted. Hastily, the most recently built residence hall, Bishop Hall, dating from 1912, was converted into an emergency hospital. There, hundreds of students were treated and unfortunately, four died. Three others died at home, making a total of seven Miami students victimized by the flu. A dozen Oxford citizens also died, and it became painfully clear that the town and campus needed a hospital.

Dr. Wade McMillan headed student health care at the time the war ended, and it was under his leadership that in 1923 a health center was finally opened on Spring Street. It was a 99-bed hospital with overnight care for students who were sick, and it would be the only hospital in Oxford until the late 1950s, when McCullough-Hyde Hospital was finally constructed. Not until the late 1970s was an agreement finally reached between the university and the town for students requiring overnight hospitalization to be treated at McCullough-Hyde, the town hospital, rather than at Wade McMillan, the university hospital. The old Wade McMillan Health Center on Spring Street has now been replaced by a new health center south of the Campus Avenue Building. The flu epidemic of 1918 brought the first hospital of any kind to Oxford, and now we have both a town hospital and a university health center.

A number of other new buildings were constructed on the Miami campus during the Hughes era. They bore such names as Wells, Gaskill, Irvin, Swing, and Ogden. Most of these names come from university trustees, though in the case of Swing Hall, the name came from David Swing, a distinguished alumnus of the class of 1852 and a faculty member at Miami before he became famous as a preacher in Chicago. Wells and Ogden Halls were built as a consequence of significant gifts.

Ogden Hall stemmed from the largest bequest in the school's history to that time, from Laura Ogden Whaling of New York City. She asked that the $250,000 gift be used to construct a women's residence hall on High Street that would bear the name of her brother, George C. Ogden, class of 1863. She also asked that it be located west of the school gymnasium, which was Herron Hall, later renamed Van Voorhis, located exactly where Ogden Hall is today. To put the new residence hall west of its present location would have put it across the street from Lewis Place, the home of the president, and the size of the building would have placed it across Slant Walk. The trustees voted to accept the terms of the bequest, on condition that the old gym be moved to the east so that the new residence hall could in fact be built west of the gym. The old gym, once called Herron Hall, later Van Voorhis, has long since been demolished, and all that is left today is a large boulder with a bronze tablet next to the Roudebush Hall parking lot, with an inscription noting that the stone and tablet mark the spot where the old gym stood until 1983, when it was finally torn down and replaced by a parking lot.

CHAPTER XIII

THE UPHAM ERA: CONTINUITY AND CHANGE

In the Hughes era, enrollment had surged from 700 students in 1911 to more than 2000 by 1927, and faculty had increased from 39 to 120 in those same years. Bishop Hall, built in 1912, was put into emergency use as a temporary hospital at the time of the savage flu epidemic in the fall of 1918. And as a result of that disastrous event, a health center was constructed on the Miami campus under the leadership of Dr. Wade McMillan, which went into service in 1923. McMillan Hall still stands on Spring Street, but it is now being used for office space primarily.

When money for Ogden Hall was given in 1923, the donor stipulated where it was to be placed on the Miami campus. The trustees were grateful for the bequest, but troubled by its location, and in order to protect Lewis Place, the home of the Miami president, and Slant Walk, the central walkway through the campus, they had to move an existing building. There are some sacred places on campus in the eyes of the trustees, and one of the most sacred is Slant Walk, which the trustees have always sought to keep clear as a green space in the center of the Miami campus. So they decided to move Herron Hall, the old gymnasium, 400 feet east, in order to build Ogden Hall west of the gym as stipulated by the donor. It was a major undertaking, but one they felt necessary to preserve Slant Walk and the view of the campus from Lewis Place.

The move wasn't an easy one, because it called for the removal of 24 giant old shade trees, and the day it was to commence, Oxford's first environmentalist, Miss Jenny Brooks, arrived to take her stand. Arms around the first tree to be cut down, she defied the ax men, saying they would have to cut her in two, since these trees were worth saving as an integral part of the university's heritage and its environment. Jenny Brooks was the daughter of a headmaster of a preparatory school in Cincinnati, and she made her point clear. The ax men dropped their axes, picked her up, repositioned her, and went on with their work. But the memory of Miss Jenny's devotion has persisted ever since, and has influenced the location of new buildings on the campus. Her concern for the beauty of the Miami campus is widely shared by alumni and townspeople, and by visitors as well, and the old trees have been preserved over the years while new ones were being planted for the future.

President Hughes not only provided for the growth in student and faculty numbers by building new classrooms and residence halls, but he provided strong leadership for the university. He took a memorable public stance in November 1920, on the occasion of the annual meeting of the National Association of State Universities and Land Grant Colleges. Miami is a state university and is one of the oldest land grant colleges in the nation, since Oxford had been earmarked as a college township by President George Washington and the Federal Congress on May 5, 1792, when John Cleves Symmes, to receive his land patent in southwest Ohio, was required to set aside a township for the support of an academy or other institution of higher learning. Every November, the National Association of State Universities and Land Grant Colleges assembles its membership, which presently numbers about 194, with one session given to presidents to share matters of major consequence occurring on their campuses.

In November of 1920, President Hughes was given four minutes to say what was happening at Miami that was of consequence. He took the opportunity to talk about a program newly launched in Oxford, calling for an Artist-in-Residence. He said that Miami's neighbor, Western College, across the highway, had already put the idea into practice, when, in 1910, it hired as a teaching member of its English faculty a woman by the name of Mrs. Jessie Kelley, whose husband was a composer of music named Edgar Stillman Kelley. She was the teacher; he was the Artist-in-Residence, with great creativity but no common sense. Edgar Stillman Kelley's major asset was his talent for writing music, dreaming of chords and variations and themes that resulted in symphonic melodies. His musical gift was recognized and the alumnae of Western College, all of whom were women, contributed funds to build a cottage for the Kelleys right on campus. This cottage still stands on the Western campus, though the college has become part of Miami University. It has a large studio which accommodated a grand piano, and Mr. Kelley used it to compose his *New England Symphony* as well as his *Pilgrim's Progress* and other musical works. Miami's President Hughes wanted to follow the example of Western College and support another Artist-in-Residence on his campus.

And so, in the spring of 1920, Miami appointed the first Artist-in-Residence at a public university, the poet Percy MacKaye. He was at the time a poet of international acclaim, and the university built what was called the Poet's Shack in the middle of the woods. The lower campus woods where the Poet's Shack once stood are surrounded today by the Bishop Oval, with buildings surrounding it. It has been allowed to resume its wild natural state as a reminder of what the campus once looked like. During his four minutes at the National Association of State Universities and Land Grant Colleges meeting in Washington, D. C., in November, 1920, Dr. Hughes explained the new Artist-in-Residence program. He argued that the patrons of the arts had once been the church, the nobility, and the wealthy citizens of a country, but the time had come for universities to become patrons of the arts.

The remarks of Dr. Hughes attracted national attention, and of all the comments made at the meeting of the association in 1920, his made the news from coast to coast. In the following decade, more than fifty other colleges and universities would follow the lead of Miami. One of the earliest was the University of Michigan at Ann Arbor, which called Percy MacKaye in Oxford and asked for a suggestion for an Artist-in-Residence on their campus. He had a poet friend, he said, who would be an admirable addition to the Ann Arbor campus, and his name was Robert Frost. The University of Michigan appointed Robert Frost as its first Poet-in-Residence. Frost later came to visit Miami to see his old friend Percy MacKaye, and he went away saying that Miami had "the prettiest campus there ever was." His words still ring true.

Over the years, Miami has been home to several poets of distinction, not only Percy MacKaye, who was a Harvard graduate, but Ridgely Torrence, who was a Miami student before he went to Princeton to finish his undergraduate degree. Ridgely Torrence had attended Miami in the 1890s, and had even published a poem in *The Miami Student* newspaper. He was invited back to campus as a faculty member in the 1920s, and later became well-known as the Poetry Editor of *The New Republic* magazine and Founder of the American Academy of Poets, which still exists. And in the tradition of these earlier Miami poets, a more recent graduate, Rita Dove, class of 1973, received acclaim as the winner of the Pulitzer Prize for Poetry in 1987, followed in 1993 by the distinction of being named the Poet Laureate of the United States. As a recent African-American woman graduate of Miami, Rita Dove continues to bring fame to Miami, where poetry has long been honored as one of the arts.

In 1927, Dr. Hughes resigned from Miami to accept the presidency of Iowa State University. He had served long and well, and was temporarily replaced by Dean Edgar Ewing Brandon for the academic year 1927-28, during which time a search was made for a permanent successor to President Hughes. The new president appointed by the trustees in 1928 was Dr. Alfred H. Upham. Alfred Upham, like Raymond Hughes, was from a farm in Preble County, north of Oxford, and both Miami graduates had been appointed to the faculty by President William Oxley Thompson, who had gone to grange meetings and farmers' institutes to recruit students for Miami. His most brilliant recruits were Hughes and Upham, both of whom had been valedictorians of their Miami classes.

Alfred Upham had come to Miami in a horse and buggy as a freshman in 1893, and graduated at the top of his class in 1897. After graduation, he accepted a brief faculty appointment to teach Greek and Latin in the preparatory school. But he went on to graduate school, first at Harvard, where he earned his master's degree, and then at Columbia, where he got his doctorate. From an initial interest in classical languages at Miami, he became more "modern" in his graduate work, taking up English language and literature as his specialty. He served briefly as a Professor of English at Utah State and then at Bryn Mawr College for women in Pennsylvania, before returning to his alma mater as a Professor of English in 1907. He would write the lyrics of "Old Miami," the Miami Alma Mater in 1907, and two years later, for the Miami Centennial, the first book-length history of the university, *Old Miami, Yale of the Early West.* During World War I, he would simultaneously teach and serve as alumni secretary for the university, and then immediately after the war, in the early 1920s, he would serve as Acting Vice-President. From there, he was called to be President of the University of Idaho, where he was serving when Miami called him to return in 1928 as the successor to President Hughes. Alfred Upham continued as President of Miami University for the next sixteen and a half years, until he was taken by death on February 17, 1945. It was the longest service of all Miami presidents, for though several have served sixteen years, only Dr. Upham served sixteen and a half years.

President Upham announced at his first meeting with the faculty that the theme of his administration would be continuity and change. There would be continuity in the preservation of the campus atmosphere, the required attendance at chapel every week, the small classes, and the personalized instruction—all reinforcing his image of the Miami he had known, when he had come in a horse and buggy to a small college of less than 200 students. Yet, while he desired continuity between the Old Miami and the New Miami, he appreciated that the university to which he returned in 1928 was already ten times larger than it had been when he came as a student in 1893. He knew Miami had to change, and it did so rapidly under his leadership. He introduced the system of Resident Advisors in the residence halls, which was not entirely new: it had begun at Miami before the Civil War, with the appointment by President Anderson of Professors Elliott and Stoddard to live in the only two residence halls on campus. But the resident advisor system that Upham started in 1929 was different, because it appointed graduate students and young instructors to be the dormitory advisors. Luckily, among the first young instructors hired specifically to be a Resident Advisor was Walter Havighurst, who became the best known writer in the university.

Walter Havighurst was no stranger to the university, because he had come out of an academic background. His father had been a professor at Lawrence University in Wisconsin, but Walter did not immediately follow in his father's footsteps. For a time he worked as a deck hand on steamships on the Great Lakes, and then, having completed a theological degree, he served an inner-city parish for the Methodist Church. It was from there that he came to Miami to be a Resident Advisor and to teach English.

Soon after he came, he met another young instructor in English, Marion Boyd, the daughter of the Western College president, whom he would marry. He also met an early Miami graduate, Joseph Bachelor, class of 1911, who had come back to Miami after having been the editor of the *Century Dictionary.* Together, Marion Boyd Havighurst and Joe Bachelor would persuade Walter Havighurst to turn his abundant talents to creative writing.

There has not been a professor quite like Walter Havighurst in all the years of Miami. I have in my personal library 36 separate volumes written by Walter Havighurst, among them *The Miami Years,* a history which he wrote for the Miami Sesquicentennial in 1959. Walter Havighurst had such a way with language that one of his students would say, "He could set your soul humming to the music of his words." He was an English teacher, but he was also an historian. He often spoke of the historian's need to see with double vision—the land as it once was, the land as it is. The fact that Walter Havighurst was one of the first Resident Advisors appointed by President Upham attests to the standard maintained by the new system.

Soon, there would be academic changes as well as residence hall changes at Miami. When Upham returned to the campus in 1928, there were two academic divisions, Liberal Arts and Education. He saw the need for a School of Business and a School of Fine Arts. The makings of a school of business were already in place, since Economics had long been a part of the Liberal Arts curriculum. The first Professor of Economics was E.S. Todd, and in 1927, after teaching economics for more than a quarter century, he was asked to lead a new School of Business Administration. Dr. Upham went on to appoint the first dean and give vigorous support to the division. He appointed as dean a man he had known at the University of Idaho, Dr. Harrison C. Dale. Dr. Dale came to Miami as the first Dean of the School of Business Administration in 1928.

Dean Dale served until 1937, when his assistant, Dean Raymond E. Glos, took over, and Dean Glos provided leadership in the Business School until 1963. Under Dean Glos, the Miami School of Business Administration would earn a reputation as one of America's finest, and he himself taught actively in it until his retirement in 1969.

Another major contributor to the reputation of Miami in the field of Business was Rollin C. Niswonger, a Miami graduate from a farming community in Darke County—Pitsburg, Ohio, it was, not Pittsburgh, Pennsylvania. Rollin Niswonger was fascinated with the subject of Accounting and was hired as the first Professor of Accounting at Miami. He wrote a textbook, *Principles of Accounting,* that is still in use across the nation. In fact, his textbook may have been the most widely used since William Holmes McGuffey produced his famous Readers a century earlier. McGuffey's Readers went to 130 million copies in print, and Niswonger's Accounting book has sold between 10 and 12 million copies. For every million copies, Rollie Niswonger received from his publisher a gold book, and in time he had a whole row of them. At the time of his death, his book controlled 68% of the national market in introductory college Accounting courses. The Miami Accounting Department is recognized today as one of the top six or seven in the country.

The School of Business Administration soon earned an outstanding reputation, and so did the School of Fine Arts. There were at first two Departments, Art and Music—though there had also been the Artist-in-Residence program that President Hughes had initiated. But the School of Fine Arts began with the Departments of Art and Music, and added Architecture. In 1928, President Upham brought another new dean with him from the University of Idaho, as he had with Dean Dale, to be the first Dean of the School of Fine Arts, Theodore Kratt. Miami now had four academic divisions within the university.

Also in 1928, a significant addition was made with the absorption of the Oxford College for Women into the university. Oxford College had been one of the three original women's colleges in Oxford, but by 1928 it had reached the end of its independent existence. Its handsome red brick building with white columns on the west side of town became a residence hall for freshmen women, later for graduate students. There are still a few graduates of the old Oxford College for Women, though their number is swiftly declining.

President Upham had to contend with a difficult legal action against the university in 1931, the celebrated Jean West case. Before then, there had never been a challenge in the courts of the right of a publicly-assisted university to suspend a student for grades. Public universities like Miami were obliged to accept graduates of public high schools, but until 1931 it had not been prevented from terminating a student for insufficient academic progress. But in 1931 Jean West, a student from a farm in Scioto County, Ohio, was denied further attendance at Miami because she had failed to make sufficient progress toward a degree. Jean West did not accept her dismissal from Miami, and, with the encouragement and support of her father, she brought suit against the university, hoping to compel Miami to allow her to continue residence until she obtained her degree. In the opinion of her father, testifying before the Court of Common Pleas in Butler County, if his daughter, Jean, didn't have the smarts to graduate, it was up to Miami to see that she got the smarts and graduated. The university's case was that it had done its best to educate her, but Jean would have to do the rest for herself. The judge at the Butler County Court of Common Pleas heard both sides in the case, and then issued an order that Miami reinstate her as a student. Miami took its argument to the Appellate Court in Cincinnati, meanwhile drawing the attention of the nation to what was happening in the courts of southwestern Ohio. If the Appellate Court upheld the decision of the Court of Common Pleas, then every public university in the country would have to reconsider its suspension of students for academic reasons. The case presented a serious challenge to the integrity of the academic profession and the degrees it offered. But in the Appellate Court, the argument of Miami University was upheld, and Jean West was not allowed to return as a student. She promptly applied to Ohio University at Athens and was accepted, thereby elevating, as one wag suggested, the academic standards of both institutions simultaneously.

In the same year that the Jean West case was heard in the courts, Miami constructed its first new building in the Upham era, Withrow Court on Talawanda Avenue. The old Herron Gymnasium had been built in 1896 for 200 students, and it was hardly sufficient for a student body which was ten times larger, having passed the 2000 mark by 1931. At the time of its dedication, Withrow Court was said, by an Ohio State Professor in his address, to be sufficient to meet the needs of Miami students for physical education, as well as for intramural and intercollegiate sports, for 100 years to come. Since then, two additions have been made to Withrow Court, and it still isn't adequate for our students, who have the newer and better facilities of Millett Hall and the new Recreation Center. Withrow Court was built in 1931, the last construction of consequence on the Miami campus until 1940, for between 1931 and 1940, the bottom fell out of the national economy, and the United States was ravaged by the Great Depression.

The Depression commenced with the stock market crash in October, 1929. There followed a recession that some thought would last only a couple of years, but in 1930, 1931, and 1932, the Depression deepened. By 1932, the public was desperate for a new direction, and turned to a presidential candidate who promised if he were elected there would be a New Deal for the American people through three Rs: Relief, Recovery, and Reform. President Franklin D. Roosevelt offered the promise of all three with his New Deal, but in spite of his election the Depression continued, with a third of the nation's families hit hard by the loss of jobs suffered by their principal breadwinners.

Miami, however, continued to grow in the decade of the 1930s, while the enrollment of many other American colleges fell. Its academic reputation brought students to Miami who might have chosen Ohio Wesleyan, Oberlin, Denison, Xavier, Wittenberg, or Marietta, because of the quality offered by a publicly-assisted university. Enrollment grew, but construction of facilities to accommodate that enrollment did not, and so classes became larger and space became tighter.

When President Roosevelt took office in 1933, he instituted the Federal Emergency Relief Administration and the National Youth Administration, helping millions of students in high schools and colleges remain in school by offering them employment. The jobs paid 25¢ an hour at first; then the pay was raised to 30¢ an hour, for such activities as cleaning blackboards, sweeping corridors, mowing grass, raking leaves, painting walls, grading papers, setting up laboratory experiments, working in dining halls, or washing dishes. One of the objectives was to keep students in educational programs as long as possible, for their own individual advantage but also for the ultimate collective advantage of the nation. The work kept them out of the job market, and they at least weren't competing with their parents for the few jobs that were available. Thousands of Miami students in the 1930s had National Youth Administration positions on campus. They stayed out of the job market for a time, and when finally the Depression was over, they were better prepared to serve society because they had remained in school and completed their education.

During the Depression years—sometimes called the Years of the Locust—President Upham was loath to accept federal funds for building construction or repair. But he did agree reluctantly to accept some funds for the rehabilitation of the two oldest residence halls, Elliott and Stoddard. Stoddard in 1936 and Elliott in 1937 would undergo major renovations, the first since their construction in the 1820s and 1830s. Public Works Administration funds were used to restore them, and the restoration can be seen under their roofs today, where the last five or six courses of brick in each building are slightly different in color from the original bricks that were used in 1828 and 1835 to build these handsome buildings. The restoration of Elliott and Stoddard Halls was the principal physical improvement to the campus in the middle years of the Great Depression.

It was not until 1940 that the country was beginning to come out of the Depression, right on the eve of World War II. World War II started in Poland and spread across the continent of Europe, and once again, the United States was not involved at first, but became heavily involved after December 7, 1941, when the Japanese suddenly bombed the United States fleet at Pearl Harbor. The Depression ended as the war began, since new jobs were emerging as we needed to provide the weapons of war, at first primarily for the Allies, England and France. It was in 1940 that Miami built its first residence halls in a long time, Symmes and Hamilton. Reflecting the manners of that earlier time, Hamilton would be built as a hall for women south of Spring Street, and Symmes would be built as a hall for men north of High Street. The sexes were still being kept apart, the women to the south end of campus, the men to the north. The center of campus was the academic area, a sort of barricade between them. Moreover, there were strict hours for the women: freshmen women were especially protected, having to be in their residences at 7:00 p.m. during the week, at 10:00 p.m. on weekends, and at 11:00 p.m. the night of the big dance. Compare those hours with what prevails on campus today—coed dormitories and visitation for both sexes in the rooms—unthinkable in 1940! Some of us still haven't adjusted to all those changes.

CHAPTER XIV

THE HERITAGE OF EXCELLENCE: "A PUBLIC IVY"

The Second World War affected Miami more than the First World War, because the United States was involved in it for almost four years rather than for a year and a half. The country was directly attacked this time, when the Japanese Navy surprised the United States fleet at its Pacific base, Pearl Harbor, Hawaii, and dealt it a heavy blow. On Dec. 8, 1941, the day after the surprise attack, President Roosevelt asked Congress to declare war on Japan, and subsequently Germany declared war against the United States, placing us in the middle of a war on two fronts that would last until 1945. In those four years of conflict, some 5,000 Miamians would serve in the military, many by enlisting, many others by being drafted, since Selective Service, as the draft was called, was already in place more than a year before the attack on Pearl Harbor. Of the 5000 Miamians in the Second World War, 150 would lose their lives. In addition, during the four years of combat, 10,000 were assigned to duty on the Miami campus by the United States Navy, for instruction in radio code, meteorology, and other special skills vital to the military effort.

The civilian enrollment at Miami dipped from approximately 3500 at the time of Pearl Harbor to just over 800 by the academic year 1943-44. Most of the remaining 800 were women, since only a handful of males were found to be 4F, that is, unfit for military service. Military enrollment, on the other hand, grew exponentially, especially after the establishment of a naval radio training school on campus on May 31, 1942. A year later, the Navy V-12 Program for training reserve officers was launched at Miami on July 1, 1943. So as Miami dormitories and classrooms were emptied of civilian students, they were filled with military personnel. By 1943-44, there were only 800 civilians, most of them women, but nearly 3000 sailors on campus, bringing the total enrollment during that year to about 3700.

The Miami faculty was equally affected. Seventy members of the Miami faculty entered military service, and another fifteen went into war-related work for the government or in private industry. Those faculty who stayed, who were mainly older, found themselves teaching courses for which they weren't prepared. Miami was assigned the preparation of radio operators for service aboard ships, and the preparation of line officers to take positions of command in the fleet. So the Miami faculty had to teach such courses as seamanship, navigation, damage control, Morse code, and semaphore—courses for which they had no prior preparation, but which they were forced to learn and teach because of the national emergency. The United States was intent on building its military strength from the ground up, into a war machine such as the world had never seen. Some 20 million Americans would serve in World War II, and even when the war was over in 1945, 12.5 million were still in uniform.

A building on the northeast corner of the Miami campus was converted into a Navy headquarters in May of 1942, when the Navy set up a radio school. It was Fisher Hall, at one time a woman's college, later an insane asylum, then a Miami men's residence hall, transformed once more during the Second World War into U.S.S. Fisher Hall. The Navy went on to add its V-12 program in July of 1943, to prepare line officers for fleet duty. Simultaneously, then, Miami was training enlisted men to be radio operators, and officers to command ships. The V-12 program used residence halls and some classroom buildings, while the Navy radio school made use of Fisher Hall for its program.

After the war, in 1946, there was a continuing presence of the military on campus, with the permanent establishment of the Naval Reserve Officer Training Corps, since Miami became one of 50 universities with a detachment of NROTC on campus. Three years later, the Air Force Reserve Officers Training Corps would establish its program at Miami. And, to further the wartime training of pilots, a Miami University Airport was installed in the summer of 1943, which is still in operation some three and one half miles west of the campus. It is not Oxford International Airport, but it provides service for Miami administrators, faculty, and staff, to go to meetings in Cleveland, Columbus, Indianapolis, Chicago, and other cities, and it forms a vital link in the Miami communication and transportation system to this day.

There was another important consequence of World War II, the Act of Congress known as the G.I. Bill ("G.I." meant all military personnel, though it originated from the initials for "Government Issue"). It was first put forward in the midst of the war, not long after landings in Normandy in 1944 made it evident that the Allies—Britain, France, and the United States—were winning. Congress addressed the compelling question of what would happen when all those who had been in military service came home. To answer the question, in the early summer of 1944, Congress passed Public Law 346, which came to be known as the G.I. Bill of Rights. The G.I. Bill guaranteed that those who wished to go to college after military service would have their way paid by the government. Many who had never aspired to a college education now had the opportunity, making the G.I. Bill one of the landmark pieces of legislation in American history. As a result of it, more than two million service men and women would go to college after the war, and Miami was one of the principal beneficiaries of the program, since thousands of former G.I.s came to Miami soon after the war ended in 1945.

The war came to a close in two stages: it ended in Europe on May 8, and in the Pacific on September 2. These events were celebrated as VE Day and VJ Day. Unfortunately, the wartime leader of the United States could not take part in either celebration, because President Franklin Delano Roosevelt died in April of 1945, and his Vice President, Harry Truman, was the head of state when Germany and Japan surrendered.

The Miami President, Alfred H. Upham, also died that year, on February 17, 1945, in his home at Lewis Place, as he was preparing a commencement address for the Women's Auxiliary Volunteer Enlisted Service Personnel, or WAVES, as they were called, who had been helping in both the radio school and the V-12 program. Alfred Upham's immediate successor was Alpheus Kasper Morris, well known as secretary and vice president of the university, who was always called by his initials, "A.K." Morris Hall was later named for him, although he served only briefly as interim president until a permanent leader could be chosen.

When that choice was made, it would be a Professor of Economics at Northwestern University, Ernest H. Hahne. Dr. Hahne had been a popular professor at Northwestern University in Evanston for many years, and was trained in business, economics and law. His area of principal expertise was public finance, an area particularly vital to a publicly-assisted university which was in the process of reconstituting itself from military to civilian status. Dr. Hahne was President of Miami University from 1946 to 1952, the post-war period, when a flood of G.I.s returned to campus, and the six years of President Hahne's administration were dominated by the effort to accommodate thousands of former service men and women coming to college.

There had been no construction during the war, and little construction in the decade of the Great Depression that preceded the war. Miami was therefore in a poor position to accommodate so many war veterans, and some quick decisions had to be made. The first decision was to convert Withrow Court into a men's residence hall. To do so meant putting double-decker bunks wall-to-wall on the basketball court, but with this Spartan accommodation, 400 men would be able to live in Withrow Court through the academic year of 1946-1947. Since many returning servicemen had seen duty in the jungles of Burma, on the islands of the South Pacific, and in the trenches of Europe, living in a double-decker bunk in Withrow Court, even if hundreds were crowded together, seemed sheer luxury.

Other quick conversions had to be made on campus. Quonset huts from the Willow Run Bomber Plant near Detroit, from Camp Perry near Port Clinton on Lake Erie, from Fort Knox and Camp Breckenridge in Kentucky, and from Fort Benjamin Harrison in Indiana were transported to the Miami campus and re-assembled as emergency housing, emergency faculty offices, emergency classrooms. Rows of temporary housing on the south campus became Veterans' Village, which was soon abbreviated to Vet Village, and later known as "Fertile Valley," when 196 married veterans moved in and started their families. Miami had never had married student housing on campus before, but many former service personnel were beyond the age of the typical college student, and needed a place for their wives and children. Vet Village became their residence on campus, an area now transformed into the handsome new Recreational Center, though the drive in front of the Recreational Center still goes by the name of Vetville Drive.

A later addition to Vet Village was called the Miami Lodges, providing additional space for about two hundred single men returning from service. These were single-story barracks located in the area where dormitories would be built later and given the names of Porter Hall,

Dodds Hall, Stanton Hall, and Anderson Hall. A barracks building, soon nicknamed "The Redskin Reservation" was put up as a temporary student union near the site of Roudebush Hall—the main administration building today, though it wasn't built until the middle 1950s. "The Res" became a popular hangout on campus in the late 1940s and early 1950s.

For many years, a proper student union had been planned, and Miami alumni had begun to contribute to it as early as the late 1930s. With the influx of thousands of veterans, a real student center had to be built, and when it finally emerged on the corner of Patterson Avenue and Spring Street, it would be called the University Center; later, the trustees would choose to rename it the Shriver Center. It replaced the familiar Redskin Reservation, but there is still a facility called "The Res" within it. The name Redskin Reservation was not a problem in 1946, though it would certainly be a problem today. By the fall of 1946, Miami enrollment had passed 4,000, half of them G.I.s, or veterans of the Second World War. Before Pearl Harbor, Miami enrollment had never topped 3500 students, but there were 4100 on campus by September 1946.

The main university architect hired to oversee the permanent campus expansion that followed the Second World War was Charles Cellarius of Cincinnati. He had designed the last two dormitories built on campus in 1940, Symmes Hall and Hamilton Hall. Now, he began to plan Reid Hall and Upham Hall, both of which were constructed in 1947 and completed in 1948. Charles Cellarius would remain the Miami architect through nearly three decades, from the late 1940s until the early 1970s. His fellow architects nicknamed him "Colonial Charlie," because he had a love affair with colonial architecture and had much to do with preserving the beauty of the Miami campus during its period of maximum expansion. It was true that his overriding interest was in colonial architecture, and his favorite American town was Colonial Williamsburg. He would spend weeks in the old capital of Virginia, studying the buildings that would be reflected on the Miami campus, and eventually he would design them.

Charles Cellarius used to say that the most important money spent on a building was the final $50,000. It was the last $50,000 that paid for the details that made the building exceptional. He took care to include such details in his plans for Miami buildings as leaded glass windows, dormer windows, bell towers, even the laying of the bricks. He wanted bricks to enhance the look of each building and complement the other buildings in appearance. He paid careful attention to the scroll work around the lighting on campus. Thanks to the work of Charlie Cellarius, the Miami campus would retain its spacious, colonial look, even after the period following the Second World War, which witnessed more construction than had ever occurred in the history of the university.

The Hahne years were the post-war years, featuring the return of the service men and women in great numbers, and, after temporary measures were taken to accommodate them, the construction of permanent buildings on campus. Dr. Hahne also took an interest in graduate education, coming as he did from Northwestern, an institution with a strong graduate program. Miami had been offering a master's degree ever since it began, in the late 1820s, awarding its first master's diploma in the commencement of 1830. But there had never been a graduate school headed by a dean. President Hahne instituted a graduate school and a dean at Miami in 1948. It was also in 1947, during the presidency of Dr. Hahne, that Miami received its largest gift of land, through the will of a faculty member and alumnus by the name of Joseph M. Bachelor.

Joe Bachelor, after graduating in 1911, had gone to work for the Century Publishing Company, publishers of the *Century Dictionary*. He became editor of the *Century*

Dictionary, and after bringing out a new edition in the middle 1920s, he came back to his alma mater to accept a position as an instructor in the English Department, and to serve as Resident Advisor in Fisher Hall along with Walter Havighurst. Joe Bachelor was, as his name suggested, a bachelor. He had proven his competence in the mastery of words as a dictionary editor. He taught a course in Shakespeare, but his favorite course was one entitled simply "Words." Miami students who enrolled in it were challenged by Joe Bachelor to add at least one word every day to their vocabulary. He told them not to go to bed at night without adding a word to their vocabulary, and then to use it until it became a natural part of their thinking. Most people, he said, use only a few hundred hackneyed words, when the English language offers thousands upon thousands of words. Joe Bachelor eventually wrote a textbook called *Words,* which was adopted by hundreds of colleges across the country.

Out of the royalties he received from his books, Joe Bachelor invested in property, mostly farmland east of the campus. He bought most of the valley of the Talawanda from the eastern edge of the campus all the way to the Oxford-Milford Road. When he died in 1947, he bequeathed his land to the university to become a wildlife preserve. Under the terms of his will, this land must remain a wilderness in the years to come, protecting the university from land development on the east. True to his wishes, the Bachelor Wildlife Preserve immediately adjacent to the campus is kept as a nature sanctuary, used only for recreation and research in the biological sciences.

It was in November, 1952, a year after the dedication of the Bachelor Wildlife Preserve, that President Hahne died of cancer, a disease which had ravaged him for years, forcing him to curtail his activities and spend much of his time in bed. The Acting President after Dr. Hahne's death was Clarence W. Kreger, a Professor of Chemistry who had been serving as Provost.

Once again, the trustees were obliged to search for a new president, and they made a distinguished choice. The new President of Miami University was John D. Millett, Professor of Public Administration at Columbia University in New York City. Dr. Millett was a graduate of DePauw University in Indiana, who had done his graduate work at Columbia, and after serving in the war, had returned to Columbia. Dr. Millett was the author of a book that was widely read by educational administrators across the country, *Financing Public Higher Education in the United States.* The problem of paying the bills was increasingly important to colleges and universities, and it made sense to bring to Miami as president an expert in the field of financial support for higher education. John Millett would serve as President of Miami for the next eleven years, from 1953 to 1964.

From Columbia, he brought with him the idea of a common curriculum for all undergraduate students. Columbia College had a liberal arts program with a core curriculum, and in 1954, the new president established a comparable program at Miami. It was his plan that all Miami students, irrespective of the division of their major, would take courses in the humanities, the sciences, and the social sciences in their freshman and sophomore years. Some choice was allowed within the Common Curriculum, but every student, whether majoring in liberal arts, education, business, or fine arts, was required to complete a certain number of core courses during the first two years. Advanced courses in major fields, or fields of personal interest, could be added during the junior and senior years. Miami had the Common Curriculum through the 1950s and 1960s, then changed it in the early 1970s to the University Requirement, and in the 1990s to what is called The Miami Plan, but in each case it has continued to be requisite for all Miami students to meet a broad liberal arts requirement in order to earn a degree.

Thus, Dr. Millett's idea of a core curriculum, which he brought with him from Columbia, is still part of a Miami education. What it means is that the School of Business Administration, or of Education, or of Fine Arts, does not merely require business courses or education courses or studio courses, but expects its students to have a liberal arts foundation in their freshman and sophomore years. John Millett was a voracious reader, a brilliant educator, and a forceful leader, who had a great vision for the future of Miami. He thought for a while of establishing an engineering program, but though the state legislature did not agree with him, he did establish a School of Applied Science in 1963, which added a fifth college to Miami University. And, through his insistence, a new program in systems analysis was introduced, one of the very first computer programs on an American college campus, as well as a program in pulp and paper science, the technology or chemistry of making paper, one of only eight such programs in the entire nation.

In 1959, President Millett led Miami in celebrating the 150th anniversary of its charter, and in that sesquicentennial year a second full-length history of the university would be written by Walter Havighurst, *The Miami Years,* which was revised and updated twice by Walter Havighurst, the last time in 1984 to mark the 175th year of Miami's chartering.

It was in the sesquicentennial year also that a new classroom building was constructed on campus, to replace the original classroom and administration building called Old Main, which had been renamed Harrison Hall in 1931. The new Harrison Hall would be constructed on the site of the old Harrison, and though its interior was significantly different, its exterior followed the outline of Old Main, with twin towers pressed against the sky as embodied in the words of the Miami Alma Mater which Alfred

Upham had written in 1903. Through John Millett's personal leadership, a Sesquicentennial Chapel was built with money contributed by Miami alumni, and it stands today on the corner of Maple and Spring, its electronic carillon often playing hymns for the campus.

After a decade as Miami president, John Millett left in 1964 to become the first Chancellor of the Ohio Board of Regents. A new governor, James Rhodes, had taken office in January, 1963, with a campaign pledge to install a public college within thirty miles of every man, woman, and child in the State of Ohio. He argued that access and choice were lacking for Ohio citizens, when there were only six public campuses in Bowling Green, Kent, Athens, Oxford, Wilberforce and Columbus. So Governor Rhodes pledged a public campus within commuting distance of every man, woman, and child within the state, and early in his administration, a Board of Regents was established by law to implement the pledge. The Ohio Board of Regents was created to be a coordinating board, not a governing board, headed by a Chancellor, whose leadership would be crucial to carrying out the master plan for higher education in Ohio. The logical choice for Chancellor of the Board of Regents was John D. Millett, President of Miami. When Dr. Millett was called away to a higher office in the late winter of 1964, Provost Charles Ray Wilson, Class of 1926 and Professor of History, served as Acting President of Miami until a permanent successor could be identified.

In the national search made by the Board of Trustees, 150 candidates applied to be Miami president, and five finalists were brought to the campus for interviews. But none of the five proved acceptable. The trustees were desperate, and decided to contact an individual who had never applied, to find out if he might be interested. The candidate received the letter from the trustees, but left it on his desk for two weeks before he answered it. Finally, he agreed to talk with them. For a couple of hours in the

Columbus Athletic Club in January, 1965, the candidate talked with the trustee search committee about the position, and then they all went to the bar. Each trustee asked for his favorite drink—a twist of this, three fingers of that, a splash of something else, light on the ice, and then the bartender turned to the candidate, who was standing there in front of him, and asked, "Young man, what would you like?" I replied, "Do you have any ice cream?" A look of astonishment crossed the bartender's face. He said he was sure he could find some somewhere in the club. What flavor did I wish? I said, "Vanilla." I didn't realize at the time what an impression it would make, but the trustees offered me the job, and for the next sixteen years, Phillip R. Shriver was President of Miami University—some said because I asked for ice cream when I was offered a drink.

I had been at Kent State University for 18 years, just 27 miles from the place where I was born, and I had never expected to leave there. I have now been at Miami for 32 years, and at Kent only 18, so that I have compiled a grand total of 50 years in higher education in Ohio, more than I ever expected to complete.

My years as Miami president, from 1965 to 1981, are now viewed as the years of the student movement. It was a movement in large measure directly opposed to the most unpopular war America has ever fought, the war in southeast Asia, centered on Vietnam. But the student movement was more than a movement against the war. It was also a movement directed towards equality: equality for the nation's minorities, long deprived of their rights as citizens, and equality for the nation's women, long kept from careers and professions. And it was a movement directed against parietal control, against the university's regulation of student conduct. Parietal rules of student conduct had been accepted on most campuses from their beginning: rules that governed behavior in class, in the dormitories, even in town, directing how one might dress, when one might leave a residence hall or return to it, when one might go home—colleges were viewed as the substitute parents of the student, and were expected to regulate student conduct.

As an example of the long-established attitude toward student behavior that prevailed before the 1960s, I can remember that every time I had a date with the woman who is now my wife, when she was at Wellesley and I was at Yale, if a date involved her absence overnight (for example, on a football weekend in New Haven where she would stay at the Taft Hotel), she had to have a written letter of permission from her parents to present to her house-mother at Wellesley, stating the time she would leave, the name of her date, where she would be staying, and the time she would return. How times have changed since then!

The student movement was in part directed against what many perceived to be the excessive regulation of student conduct by universities and colleges. It was unfortunate that much of the movement came to be directed against the war, but that cause attracted most of the attention in the press. Miami had both a Navy and Air Force Reserve Office Training Corps on campus, and a confrontation between students—who were exempted from the draft to go to college—and the U.S. military presence on campus was inevitable. It all came to a head in the spring of 1970. The student movement had started on the West Coast and spread to the East Coast, then worked its way into the Midwest. Its first major effort was a Free Speech movement at the University of California at Berkeley in March of 1964. By 1968, it had spread to the East Coast, especially to Columbia University, where the office of President Grayson Kirk (Miami Class of 1924) was occupied for five days by students. By 1969, and, particularly, by the spring of 1970, when the Vietnam War was carried into neighboring Cambodia, the Midwest exploded with anti-war protests on its college campuses.

At Miami, there was a student sit-in at Rowan Hall, the

building facing the Sesquicentennial Chapel, which was at the time our Naval ROTC Headquarters. (Today, partly as a result of that sit-in, the Headquarters of both the Navy and Air Force ROTC are located in the basement of Millett Hall.) There was also, not long after the sit-in at Rowan Hall, the so-called "flush-in" which affected not only the Miami campus but the entire Oxford community. I don't know to this day who had that "brilliant" idea, but here it was: Turn on all the faucets, flush all the toilets, and turn on the showers—all at precisely 6:00 p.m. In 25 minutes, the entire water supply of the City of Oxford had gone down the drain. The reservoirs were empty, and it was impossible to drain millions of gallons through small four and six inch pipes. The end result was that the water had to go somewhere, and where it went was the basements of Oxford. I'll never forget the call I had that evening from a well-known local physician, Dr. Bill Beck, telling me that the water was up to the piano keys in his basement recreation room.

If any single event brought a halt to excessive student protests at Miami in the spring of '70, it was the "flush-in," because immediately everybody was inconvenienced. People began to be thirsty, but there was no water to drink. They wanted to have a shower, but no water came out of the shower head. They wanted to flush their toilets, but nothing happened. About midnight, people began to wonder, what do we do in case of fire? We have no water to put the fire out. So the earlier public sympathy aroused by the sit-in at Rowan Hall was more than countered by the adverse public reaction to the flush-in.

In that troubled spring of 1970, 720 American colleges closed. Miami was one of them; we closed for a week. When we reopened, we had 930 students standing guard in campus buildings and 50 faculty members serving as officers of the watch, aware that one night during the student protests at Kent State, seven fires had been set on campus. The spring of 1970 was the low point of student morale and the high point of student distress during the Vietnam War, and afterwards, fortunately, the Miami campus quieted down.

During my sixteen years as President of Miami, not all our time was given to the student movement: doctoral programs were introduced in ten different fields of study, branch campuses came into being at Middletown and Hamilton, and in 1968 a European study center was installed in the Grand Duchy of Luxembourg. This Luxembourg campus is now called the John E. Dolibois European Center of Miami University, in honor of a Miami alumnus who had come to the United States as an immigrant, unable to speak, read, or write English, and who had returned to his native Luxembourg fifty years later as United States Ambassador. John Dolibois had served as Vice President for Development and Alumni Affairs at Miami during the 1960s and the 1970s, and in the 1980s he went back to Luxembourg as Ambassador.

In 1967, a joint campus was started by Ohio State and Miami in the Dayton area, Miami providing the faculty in the humanities, and Ohio State the faculty in the sciences, the two universities together creating a new university called Wright State. It was the first instance of a joint action by two public universities in Ohio to start a new university that would become independent of both.

Of importance, from 1965 to 1981, 45 buildings were added to the Miami campus, 30 of them new and 15 old. The thirty new buildings included Millett Hall, King Library, the Center for Performing Arts, the Hughes Laboratories, and the Marcum Conference Center. The fifteen old buildings were acquired when Western College became part of Miami in 1974. With the merger of Miami and Western, at long last the process by which a town of colleges had become a college town was complete: there was one university where once there had been five colleges.

Some argued that with the merger Western should become a law school, and serious consideration was given to that possibility. Others advocated that the Western campus should become a shopping center. But fortunately, the decision was made with warm support from the faculty to create a new division of the university, a School of Interdisciplinary Studies. Today, the Western College program is the School of Interdisciplinary Studies, opening up opportunities for students to devise their own courses of study with faculty supervision, and to major in more than a single academic discipline. It was in 1978, four years after Western College became part of Miami, that the Higher Education Research Administration (HERA) published a report in Los Angeles commending Miami for the establishment of its new division, and taking note of the fact that Miami was now to be ranked among the top twenty publicly supported institutions in the nation for the overall excellence of its programs and its students.

Further honors came to Miami in the field of athletics. From 1964 to 1989, Richard G. "Dick" Shrider served as Director of Athletics, including sixteen years when the university would be acknowledged as having the best athletic program in the Mid-American Conference. From 1973 to 1975, Miami football reached the peak of its achievement: three consecutive seasons with 32 wins, 1 loss, and 1 tie. The loss and tie were both to Big Ten teams: Miami lost to Michigan State 14-13, and tied Purdue 7-7. Each of those three winning seasons ended with a trip to a New Year's Bowl game. Miami was victorious in all three bowl games, first over the University of Florida, then over the University of Georgia, and finally over the University of South Carolina, and it was ranked in the top ten teams in the nation in Division 1A football.

In basketball, Miami teams also did well, especially the 1978 basketball team, which earned a berth in the NCAA finals and in the first round defeated defending national champion Marquette in the Market Square Arena in Indianapolis. The captain of that winning Miami squad was Randy Ayers, later to become head coach of the Ohio State basketball team.

The Shriver presidency at Miami came to an end in 1981, when I resigned to return to the classroom as Professor of History, and was replaced by Paul Pearson, a Professor of Zoology who came to Miami from Rutgers, the State University of New Jersey, where he had been serving as executive vice president and then acting president. In the eleven years of Paul Pearson's presidency, Yager Stadium was built in 1983, replacing the old Miami Field, and a new Biological Sciences building was erected, which in time would be appropriately named Pearson Hall in his honor. It was in the Pearson years, too, in 1985, that Richard Moll, Director of Admissions at the University of California, published a book entitled *The Public Ivys,* in which he argued that there were eight publicly-assisted universities in the nation which rivaled the eight Ivy League universities. The eight "Public Ivys" were the University of California at Berkeley, the University of Texas at Austin, the University of Michigan at Ann Arbor, the University of Virginia at Charlottesville, the University of North Carolina at Chapel Hill, William and Mary at Williamsburg, the University of Vermont at Burlington, and Miami University at Oxford, Ohio.

When President Pearson retired in 1992, after 11 years in office, his place was taken by Paul G. Risser, a Professor of Botany who came to us from the University of New Mexico where he had been executive vice president and provost. His time with us was short, but during his three years, a campus-wide computer network would be initiated which would ultimately link every student room and every classroom on campus. Paul Risser left in 1995 to go to Oregon State as president. Following the acting presidency of the Provost, Dr. Anne Hopkins, a new president was appointed in 1996, James C. Garland, a Professor of Physics and Dean at Ohio State.

Dr. Garland had been executive dean of the Colleges of Arts and Science at Ohio State, presiding over five separate Colleges of Arts and Science in that very large university. As an auspicious prelude to his administration, *The Miami Student* in 1995 published the headline, "Miami Ranks Nationally," over a lead article which reported that *U.S. News & World Report* for September 18, 1995, ranked the national universities preeminent in undergraduate instructional programs: leading the list was Dartmouth, then came Brown, William and Mary, Rice, Princeton, Stanford, Duke, and then Miami University, Oxford, Ohio, followed in 9th place by Notre Dame and in 10th place by Yale University.

Our first president, Robert Hamilton Bishop, had a dream that some day Miami would be the Yale of the West. I think that if he were to return to campus today, Robert Hamilton Bishop would be both pleased and proud to see how far Miami has come toward realizing that dream.

Index

D

I

J

K

L

M